The New Short-Term Therapies for Children

A guide for the helping professions and parents

Lawrence E. Shapiro, Ph.D.

A SPECTRUM BOOK

Prentice-Hall, Inc., Englewood Cliffs, New Jersey 07632

Library of Congress Cataloging in Publication Data

Shapiro, Lawrence E.
  The new short-term therapies for children.

  "A Spectrum Book."
  Bibliography: p.
  Includes index.
  1. Child psychotherapy.   2. Psychotherapy, Brief.
I. Title.
RJ504.S517   1984   618.92'8914   84-6871
  ISBN 0–13–615724–6
  ISBN 0–13–615716–5 (pbk.)

Manufacturing: Doreen Cavallo
Production coordination: Inkwell

This book is available at a special discount when ordered
in bulk quantities. Contact Prentice-Hall, Inc., General
Publishing Division, Special Sales, Englewood Cliffs, N.J. 07632.

10 9 8 7 6 5 4 3 2 1
Printed in the United States of America

ISBN 0-13-615724-6

ISBN 0-13-615716-5 {PBK.}

Prentice-Hall International, Inc., *London*
Prentice-Hall of Australia Pty. Limited, *Sydney*
Prentice-Hall Canada Inc., *Toronto*
Prentice-Hall of India Private Limited, *New Delhi*
Prentice-Hall of Japan, Inc., *Tokyo*
Prentice-Hall of Southeast Asia Pte. Ltd., *Singapore*
Whitehall Books Limited, *Wellington, New Zealand*
Editora Prentice-Hall do Brasil Ltda., *Rio de Janeiro*

Contents

Introduction

THE BIRTH OF A SHORT-TERM THERAPIST

Nearly a decade ago, when I was a school psychologist in a rural school district in Colorado, I believed that open-ended, individual psychotherapy with children was the only way to have a significant impact on their problems. I had arrived in Colorado by way of very rewarding psychoanalytic training in New York City, where I had been fascinated with the slow unravelling of the Gordian Knot of the psyche that characterizes the analytic mode of therapy. Watching the human mind unfold, delicately revealing its layers in the security of a therapeutic relationship, was a sublime experience whether it was with children, adolescents, or adults. I had learned the rewards of patience and empathic caring built on an unhurried acceptance of the way children reveal themselves.

In Colorado, I inherited a caseload of 150 children with identified emotional and learning problems. For a year, I bemoaned the insufficient resources and stop-gap services that I felt I was providing. Since I wore many hats in providing psychological services in six different schools, I rarely had more than ten children in individual therapy, and those I saw only once a week for one-half hour, and usually for no more than three- or four-month stretches. Believing that intensive individual therapy was the only legitimate form of psychotherapy, I assumed that I was only doing "crisis-intervention"—putting out one fire while on the way to the next. I treated the most severe cases first, and when their problems were somewhat abated, I would work my way down the referral list to the less immediate problems, hoping that the children I had just worked with, although obviously not "cured," would at least have their problems stay in remission. Oddly enough, many of these children did improve, although I wasn't sure why. Watching children improve their behavior, feel better about themselves, or adjust to difficulties at home without having gone through months or years of therapy had a profound effect on me.

With limitations of time and space, I had to completely reconceptualize my ideas about therapy. Since I worked in empty broom-closets and in the back of gymnasiums instead of well-equipped play-therapy rooms with two-way mirrors, I usually carried all my materials in a large box. Fortunately, either the clean Colorado air or my youth had made me much more open to experimentation.

While I was completing my doctoral work, I became interested in the applications of developmental psychology to psychotherapy with children, and began devising my own games that focused on specific developmental/emotional problems of children (see The Developmental

Game Technique, Chapter 7). I even flirted with behavioral techniques, although I didn't admit this at the time to my analytic mentors and colleagues back in New York.

But still I never felt that I had enough time to do things right; this made me feel insecure and defensive about my work. I always felt on the verge of exhaustion, and though I had hardly begun my professional career, I began to show the signs of "job burnout," a syndrome familiar to many therapists who work in schools, public clinics, and other institutional settings. Fortunately, I persevered, always convinced that the system could be changed to provide more resources for children and to give therapists who worked in the public field more time to do their jobs.

Then, after many more years of griping about inadequate resources in several different jobs, I finally began to accept a truth that had escaped me: There will never be enough time and resources to give the large majority of children long-term individual therapy. But there are other ways to help children change. We can create new techniques or modify old ones so they are more effective in a shorter amount of time. We can use other people—parents, teachers, or paraprofessionals—to fulfill many of the therapeutic needs of children. We can develop a really creative system of diagnosis and treatment that focuses precisely on the nodal change points of a child's life, and stimulates development far beyond the time he or she spends with the therapist.

HOW TO USE THIS BOOK

The purpose of short-term therapy is to have the greatest impact on a child's problems in the shortest possible amount of time; the purpose of this book is to suggest ways that this can be done. Chapter 1 is an attempt to define the important characteristics of short-term psychotherapy for children, in contrast to traditional long-term psychodynamic approaches. Chapter 2 presents a model for conceptualizing effective time-limited therapy, stressing the need for comprehensive pre-therapy planning and a multitechnique approach. The remainder of the book is devoted to techniques, for I think what most therapists and prospective therapists are interested in reading about are practical applications.

In Chapters 3 through 11, I have focused on the clinical application of the techniques, rather than on their development or the theories behind them. Many of the therapeutic interventions that I discuss can be found in anthologies, which are useful in giving an overview for the student of psychotherapy, but are not that helpful for the clinician. In anthologies each chapter is written by either the originator of a therapy or some other prominent theorist who exclusively practices child psychotherapy from that one point of view. But most therapists I know do not just subscribe to one school of therapy or one set of techniques; they are constantly experimenting with new approaches and trying to meaningfully integrate these into their practices. The integration of these techniques is what this book is about.

For more than a dozen years I have grappled with the application of diverse schools of thought and methodologies for helping children at a time when there have been many changes and wide experimentation in our field. The result is a system for looking at children's problems and trying to match them with effective therapeutic techniques. (I stress that this is a system for many diverse techniques, not the system). It is my hope that by presenting my own work as a model, complete with my prejudices, wisdom, mistakes, and successes, I might inspire other therapists to do the same.

The effectiveness of any treatment program will always lie in the ingenuity, intellect, talent, and capacity for caring in the therapist, rather than in the techniques themselves. If I can inspire any therapist to think about the ways that he or she chooses and applies the vast number of interventions that are available, then I will have accomplished my purpose in writing this book.

I present the techniques in this book from my very opinionated viewpoint, and I am sure in many cases have done some disservice to their original authors and to practitioners who specialize in just one set of techniques. Similarly, I have made no attempt to give each school of therapy equal time, for I give some techniques much more weight in my practice than others. A chapter on family therapy was omitted from the final version of this book due to lack of space for an adequate discussion of these techniques, however, in practice, I use family therapy techniques with nearly every case. The family therapy models of Jay Haley (1973, 1976) and Salvador Minuchin (1974) are particularly relevant to short term therapy with children. For a comprehensive overview of the field, see the *Handbook of Family Therapy*, edited by Gurman and Kniskern (1981).

If you pick up this book with a particular child or therapeutic problem in mind, then you will probably not find yourself reading it straight through. You may want to simply thumb through it and see what catches your eye; I have provided, however, several ways to help make your search for specific information more fruitful.

First, you will find that each chapter is introduced by three paragraphs indicating the type of psychological problems that I find most often respond to each group of techniques, specific indicators that might heighten the therapeutic effect, and contraindications that might prohibit the use of a technique with particular types of children. Again, I must remind the reader that these guidelines are extremely subjective, based for the most part on my own experience and analysis of clinical studies. The practice of psychotherapy would be greatly enriched if we had the objective data from tightly designed comparative research to accurately guide us in choosing which techniques will work with which kids, but this data does not exist. The research comparing the effectiveness of different techniques has been exceptionally thin, and most of what is available is inconclusive. Furthermore, the complex methodological problems in designing such studies lends doubt as to whether such information will ever be available to therapists. So instead, I offer my clinical judgment, knowing its limitations and hoping that each therapist will filter my recommendations through his or her own experience and knowledge.

There are two indices that are designed to help the reader find specific techniques. The first, found in Appendix A, is a list of the case examples used in the book, alphabetized by type of treatment, each with a reference to identifying characteristics of the child and the presenting problem in each example (such as, "biofeedback for an adolescent girl with migraine headaches"). After reading a case example to get a flavor for whether or not a specific technique would be appropriate for the child you have in mind, go back and read the entire chapter or section. This will help you get a broader perspective on the principles behind each technique, compare related techniques, and find references for further reading. Finally, Chapter 2 provides an Assessment Matrix (p. 19), a quantitative system for selecting specific strategies for a multiple-technique treatment plan. The Assessment Matrix suggests how a child's strengths and weaknesses in 65 diagnostic areas would guide the therapist toward selecting the major techniques and therapies in this book.

ON LANGUAGE

For some time the field of psychology has been criticized for using language that clouds the issues rather than clears them up. Although there has been little revision of the language in existing theories, there has been a tendency for newer therapies to be conceptualized in plainer English. But still it seems inevitable that each new therapy will introduce a few dozen new terms and redefine a few dozen old ones. This presents a particular problem for therapists who use the multiple-treatment approach that this book advocates.

As much as possible I have tried to avoid the use of esoteric psychological language and have tried to present concepts as simply as possible. However in many therapies, particular words imply a richness of meaning that is difficult to define outside the theoretical constructs of that school of thought. The reader can assume that when I am talking about a particular technique or therapy, I am using language as it exists in the context of that system, unless otherwise noted.

I'd also like to make note of a few other uses of language. I have tried to use both the masculine and feminine pronouns to refer to both therapists and clients, and to avoid sexist stereotypes. To provide more fluent reading, I have often used the word "child" to refer to both children and adolescents, but when a particular technique or idea applies only to a specific age group—infants, toddlers, pre-schoolers, elementary school-age children, early, mid, or late adolescents—this will be indicated by noting the specific age range. In other instances, the word "children" implies no specific age connotation and the reader may assume that I am referring to adolescents as well.

Finally, let me mention certain liberties I have taken with the language of other authors for the sake of clarity and consistency in this book. Often when an author invents a new technique, he or she automatically pronounces it a new therapy, when in fact, it is actually based on the principles of an already established school of thought. As a result we have hundreds of "new therapies" to confuse the clinician. For example, in the chapter entitled the Video Self-Modeling Technique, I refer almost exclusively to the work of Betsy Haarmann and Mike Greelis, authors and creators of what they call Video Therapy (Greelis and Haarmann, 1980). But what they have developed is actually a system of ingenious techniques based on behavioral principles, not a new therapy in itself. My term, "video self-modeling technique," is more descriptive of the principles that the technique is based on. In other instances, I may have not stressed the use of certain language the way the original authors of the therapy or technique might have intended. For a broader understanding of the language and constructs of any particular therapy, I refer the reader back to the original sources or to anthologies.

WHERE TO GO FROM HERE

It is my hope that this book will serve as a starting point for child psychotherapists or students of psychotherapy to think about how they help children, and particularly about how they can integrate the plethora of techniques and theories available to them into a systematic clinical practice. This is not an instruction book on how to do the therapies and techniques that are presented, but a model for how to think about putting them together. To use the majority of these techniques effectively will take some additional reading and training. Fortunately, workshops, seminars, and conferences are held year round throughout the country in nearly every school of therapy that I have mentioned. Another route therapists take to develop their skills is to seek postgraduate supervision. I recently talked to an experienced therapist who, in order to keep up with the latest techniques, periodically consulted supervisors in widely different therapeutic modalities.

The practice of psychotherapy has extraordinary rewards, but it is also a complex and emotionally exhausting profession. Helping others grow demands constant growth by the therapist as well, and I hope that readers can take advantage of every opportunity to expand their horizons while maintaining a sense of who they are and what they do well. If this book can contribute in any small way to that goal, it will have served my intent.

ACKNOWLEDGMENTS

The material in this book covers over a dozen years work with children in which time I have been privileged to work with and be trained by many professionals from the various fields of mental health. All who have nourished my creativity as a psychotherapist and have given me support to experiment and take risks.

To begin chronologically, I would like to acknowledge the help and guidance of Blanche Saia, my advisor at the Bank Street College of Education, and Bernice Burke, who supervised my first internship at the Bank Street Lab School. The dedication of these two women inspired me early in my work and provided me with a basic understanding of therapeutic caring and advocacy for children that has largely shaped my career. Next I would like to thank two people for their encouragement and guidance in the next stage of my training: Betty Meyer of the Douglas County School System, and Steve Hodge of the University of Colorado at Boulder. From Betty Meyer I received unquestioning belief in my ability and talent that gave me the nerve to continually experiment with new ways to help children, teachers, and families. But more important, for two years I sat and walked in the aura of her compassion toward generations of children in her community—a compassion that seemed boundless. From Steve Hodge, my doctoral advisor, I received quiet, steady support to guide my career.

At the National Children's Center, Inc. in Washington, D.C., I received support from many people in developing new techniques to work with the mentally handicapped. In particular, I would like to thank the Executive Director, Sam Orenstein, for encouraging my resourcefulness in developing programs for multi-handicapped children and to Howie Smith, my friend and colleague, who more than anyone else has supported my attempts at writing. I would also like to acknowledge the talent and help of several of the therapists that I supervised at the National Children's Center, most notably, Liz Loden, Ron Golkow, and Sherry Vavrichek. Several of the clinical examples presented in this book are composites from cases where they were the primary therapists. These have influenced many of my ideas by their feedback and their own experimentation.

I am indebted to Betsy Haarmann and her husband, Mike Greelis, for introducing me to Video Therapy (see Chapter 6), a technique that continues to fascinate me with its implications for treating clients who would be extremely resistant to less exciting types of therapy. Betsy worked with me in my first efforts at using this technique and Mike was kind enough to "walk me through" my first experience in a video-editing lab.

With deep admiration, I would like to acknowledge the help and guidance of Rochelle Kainer who supervised my work when I was very much in need of a refined and careful listener. Her insight and caring had a profound influence on my efforts to integrate diverse professional training and experience.

I would like to gratefully thank my wife, Deborah Lamb, who contributed in many ways toward the successful completion of this book. Trained as a creative arts therapist, Deborah has greatly influenced my appreciation of the various art modalities and helped write Chapter 8. Deborah also painstakingly edited many of the other sections of this book for both style and content, making it a much more readable work.

Finally, there are many parents of the children and adolescents I have treated whom I would like to acknowledge for their influence on my career and personal growth. Although I cannot name them—and there are too many to name anyway—I would like to thank them for their inspiration in dealing with some of the most difficult of life's circumstances. In the worst of times they have not given up loving and caring for their children, making sacrifices, and going on. Many of the parents I have worked with, particularly the parents of severely handicapped children, have scaled the heights of human dignity. To play even a small part in helping them has given me immense satisfaction.

Lawrence E. Shapiro

1

Toward a Definition of Short-Term Therapy

This is a book for people who help kids. It is aimed primarily at professional therapists, such as social workers, psychiatrists, psychologists, nurses, and counselors, but it may also be valuable for regular classroom teachers, parents, and grandparents. Anyone who spends time with children can be part of their learning and growth and can provide therapeutic advice, guidance, experiences, and structure.

As the reader shall see, there are many ways to do "therapy" with children, from reading books, playing games, drawing, and dancing, to using sophisticated behavioral and even electronic technologies. While some of these techniques require both natural ability and specialized training, many others require only that the person working with the child be sensitive, and caring, and know about a few principles of helping children learn to help themselves.

For years it was assumed that the only people who could do therapy with children were the ones working in a private practice or clinic with a room full of therapeutic toys and games, and years of experience in psychoanalytically oriented play therapy. This kind of treatment often took several years. But while this method of treatment may be still appropriate for children with certain types of problems, the reality is that most children who get help from a therapist receive it in a relatively brief time period and in all sorts of situations. I arbitrarily define short-term therapy as lasting 25 hours or less, over a period of six months or less. Sometimes the goals of therapy can be accomplished in only an hour or two with a professional, and sometimes the child need not see a professional therapist at all. Therapy can take place virtually anywhere.

There are many reasons why children are commonly seen for a period of weeks or months, rather than a period of years. The obvious one is economics. Even with health insurance, long-term psychotherapy can run into thousands of dollars a year. Another reason is the proliferation of mental health professionals who are trained to work with children. Child development and child psychology courses are now standard in scores of undergraduate and graduate programs that train people for work in schools, hospitals, daycare centers, community based health centers, and churches. But perhaps the most important impetus for the changes in how we help children is the changing attitudes of parents. Through the news media, books, and workshops, mothers and fathers have been educated to recognize the early signs of problems their children are having, and the stigma of seeking help has lessened considerably. Life is tough these days for both children and their parents, and we are all beginning to see that there is no need to suffer in silence.

Accepting the fact that most children who are seen in psychotherapy will receive treatment over a relatively short period of time, how can we make sure that every moment of therapy is as effective as it can be? There are hundreds of therapy techniques from which to choose, but which ones will work most efficiently for each child? What is the best way to help a child get over recurrent nightmares? What do you do with a child who is angry all the time or one who fights with his sister so much that the family can't even eat a meal together? What about the child who is fearful or shy and has no friends? Ask these questions to three different therapists and you are likely to get three different answers.

Many therapists today deal with the overabundance of psychological theories and techniques by explaining that they have an eclectic point of view, which is based in a particular school of thought, but also takes into account the immediate needs of the patient. But as Lazarus (1980) has pointed out, this often means that the therapist chooses techniques largely on a basis of his/her subjective judgment operating on the premise: "I use whatever makes sense to me and whatever I feel comfortable with." Quoting Eysenk (1970), Lazarus argues that this intuitive approach to therapy ends up to be "a mish-mash of theories, a hugger-mugger of procedures, a gallimaufry of therapies . . . incapable of being tested or evaluated."

To deal with this confusion, Lazarus promotes a "systematic eclecticism," called Multi-Modal Therapy, which defines seven areas in which patients express their problems and draws upon a variety of techniques to address each area in turn. Lazarus notes that while theories may be basically incompatible (e.g., behaviorism vs. psychoanalysis), techniques are not. He advocates that a thorough diagnosis can be translated into a treatment plan which can use several techniques simultaneously, depending on the needs and style of the patient. This plan should take into account seven modes—behavior affect, sensation, imagery, cognition, inter-personal skills, drugs, and health—that form the acronym BASIC I.D.

However, while Lazarus emphasizes the need to treat the patient in seven different modalities, I believe that the effectiveness behind his therapy has more to do with the use of multiple techniques, which can be chosen in any systematic fashion based on a thorough diagnostic assessment.

The use of multiple techniques is particularly appropriate in short-term therapy where the object is to maximize the therapeutic effect in the least amount of time possible. One successful therapist has explained his use of a multiple-method therapy as a "shotgun approach" —firing many missiles simultaneously at the target hoping that at least one will hit the bulls-eye. But this analogy assumes that the "shots" are independent of each other, and while one or two may hit dead center, most will miss. I prefer to think that the use of multiple techniques has a synergistic effect, with each technique working interdependently with the others, so that the total therapeutic impact is even greater than the sum of its parts.

While I agree with much of what Lazarus has to say about the need for a systematic eclecticism, I would never call myself a Multi-Modal Therapist. Coming from a behavioristic background, Lazarus rightly emphasizes exacting diagnostic assessment to determine which techniques should be used with each individual client. But he then assumes that once the techniques have been identified, any well trained therapist can carry them out, and here I disagree. This assumption undoubtedly originates in Lazarus's experience in behaviorism, a school of therapy which deemphasizes the personality and intuitiveness of the therapist. But other therapies emphasize certain innate characteristics of the therapist, such as creativity, warmth, and spontaneity, which we do not all possess in equal amounts. While Lazarus urges that the individuality of each patient be respected down to his/her language and style, he neglects to see that the therapist's individual training, experiences, tastes, interests, and personality must also be accounted for in the therapy. Every therapist is different, just as every patient is different, and we must use the uniqueness of both in the therapy. To be effective therapists we must know our strengths and weaknesses, as well as those of our clients.

Ideally, a short-term therapist is a consummate craftsman, sharing characteristics with at least three other professions. First of all, short-term therapists are premier detectives. They consider every nuance, not only of the child's personality, but also of the "personality" of the child's world. They understand all aspects of their client's development, and how it may be impeded by the presenting problem. They understand how the child's family system has contributed to the problem, both positively and negatively, and how the child's problems affect his time in school, where he spends more than a quarter of his waking hours. Second, short-term therapists are brilliant chemists, always searching for the right ingredients to catalyze change and growth in the child's life. And like chemists, they combine the creativity of art and the preciseness of science, always searching for the nodal points where just the right additions or subtractions will make the difference. And finally, they are four star chefs, preparing a "course" of therapy nearly perfect in its attention to detail. Thoroughly trained to heighten their perceptions, they never throw together just what is on hand, but prepare for each step well in advance. They use assistants, naturally, to help in the preparation, and to serve with precision what has been prepared. And the final product is almost like a work of art—appealing to every sense, nutritious, easy to digest, and of course, delectable.

THE DIFFERENCE BETWEEN SHORT AND LONG TERM THERAPY

The difference between short- and long-term therapy is more than a matter of time. They are two distinct models of psychotherapy with some similarities, but more divergence

The therapist and the child are usually best served when short-term therapy is most broadly defined. The aim of short-term therapy is not to "cure" children, but rather to stimulate their internal resources for growth and development and to simultaneously make their environment more responsive to their needs. Short-term therapy is rarely an end in itself, but rather a transition point in a child's journey towards adulthood.

While long-term therapy is usually open-ended and deliberately ambiguous about its purpose, short-term therapy seeks to define the child's problem in as concrete terms as possible. Through thorough diagnostic assessments, the therapist formulates hypotheses about the change points in the child's inner and outer life. A written plan is used to conceptualize the entire course of the therapy including not only the specific goals and objectives to be accomplished, but also the specific techniques that will be used to achieve them. Because the therapy is time-limited, the techniques that the therapist will choose to achieve each goal will contain as much therapeutic "power" as possible.

Long-term therapists typically use non-directive and reflective techniques which allow children to reveal their conflicts and their solutions at their own rate. They create a nonjudgmental and accepting atmosphere where the children can explore the underlying, unconscious issues that created their problems. However, the short-term therapist, with only a finite period of time for treatment, takes a more systematic approach. Based on a creative battery of standardized and non-standardized measures and with information provided from the child's family and other correspondents, the therapist identifies the most important problems to be solved. These in turn are ranked hierarchically and become the major focus of the treatment.

A major difference in short-term therapy is its approach to the treatment of symptoms. A long standing psychoanalytic premise, which began as a response to the behavioral movement of the 1950's and 1960's, has been that if you treat the surface manifestation of a problem without resolving the underlying conflict, then another symptom, a potentially more serious one, would promptly take its place. But after more than two decades of treating the overt behaviors of children, this caveat has not been supported by clinical practice. Moreover, the concept of "symptom removal" is itself a misnomer. A psychotherapist is not a dentist extracting parts of a personality that are no longer useful. No form of therapy is so powerful that it can change a child in ways that are incompatible with his or her basic needs. The goal of all psychotherapy is to give children choices where before they had none. Short-term therapies seek to do this in the most expedient way possible by showing children how to use their inner resources more adaptively and how to make their external world more receptive to change. If a symptom functions in an adaptive way for the child that the therapist does not foresee, then the child will maintain that symptom until he can see that another way of functioning will serve him better. While short-term therapy may occasionally fail to change a child in the direction that the therapist would like, it would be highly unlikely that it could make a child worse. Some specific exceptions, where short-term therapy would be contraindicated, will be considered later in this chapter.

Moreover, many systems therapists have rejected the medical model of symptoms and diseases altogether. Jay Haley (1976), who uses a directive approach to family therapy, considers all psychological problems to be a repeating sequence of acts between several people, maintaining the particular way that they relate to each other. He states that what we refer to as a symptom, such as a phobia or depression, is simply a "label for the crystallization of a sequence in a social organization." The child's behavior is seen as a metaphor for larger problems in the family, usually between the parents, and when the dynamics of the family system change, the child's "symptoms" disappear.

As we shall see in later chapters, "symptomatic" behaviors may even be part of the treatment process where one symptom can be used to compete or nullify the other, or an innocuous symptom can be substituted for another more serious one (see Chapter 4, Innovative Individual Behavioral Approaches).

While this book emphasizes the new techniques available to the short-term therapist for promoting effective change, some issues and techniques of more traditional therapy, including the roles of transference, counter-transference, and resistance, may also play a role in short-term therapy.

Transference, the projection of the client's inner feelings, images, and representations onto the therapist, occurs in every type of psychotherapy whether it is recognized and interpreted or not. As in long-term traditional therapy, the recognition and use of the transference phenomenon as a specific technique will vary according to the training and orientation of the therapist. Therapists who have been schooled in psychoanalytic methods will pay more attention to this technique than humanistic therapists who have a "here and now" orientation. Some of the techniques described in this book, such as hypnotherapy and transactional analysis, rely heavily on the transference phenomenon because the techniques are built on a psychoanalytic tradition. But other methods, such as reality therapy or biofeedback, will ignore the phenomenon altogether.

Counter-transference, the projection of the therapist's needs and conflicts onto the client, is an issue which must be dealt with no matter what the orientation of the therapist or what techniques are being used. To be effective, therapists must recognize when their objectivity is colored by their needs and prejudices. This is certainly not to say that therapists shouldn't have all the feelings and foibles of the human condition, but rather that these must be recognized and kept out of the therapy, unless it serves some therapeutic purpose to reveal them. Certain methods, such as reality therapy and values clarification, encourage therapists to be self-disclosing as part of the therapeutic process. However, even with these methods the therapist's personal thoughts, feelings, and experiences are not revealed randomly as in social conversation, but are selectively chosen and judiciously used as in any other treatment technique.

Resistance is commonly defined as the various defense mechanisms that the client uses in order to protect him/herself from self-awareness. But I prefer to use an expanded definition of this concept, as suggested by Gardner (1975), to include anything that prevents the client from participating in the therapeutic process. Unlike the psychoanalytic therapist who limits his intervention to the interpretation of resistance, the short-term therapist meets obstacles to therapeutic change more directly. But directness does not necessarily mean confrontation. From the inception of the therapy plan, the therapist seeks to ally himself or herself with the child by choosing techniques which are compatible with his/her interests and style. The desire of the therapist to have the child accept the treatment process rather than fight it is one of the major determinants by which therapy techniques are chosen. For example, a child interested in video games and space age technology might be drawn towards the electronic gadgetry used in biofeedback. Children who have difficulty expressing themselves in words might be more open to the nonverbal techniques of dance or music therapy. A psychologically sophisticated adolescent, who wants to compete with the therapist in dealing with his problem or the problems in his family,

may be introduced to transactional analysis which has translated sophisticated psychological concepts into concrete terms and which emphasizes the ability of clients to be their own therapists.

THE PARTICIPATION OF OTHERS IN THE THERAPY

Most short-term therapists are more "social" than their long-term traditional counterparts. At every stage of the treatment the short-term
therapist interacts with other adults in the child's life to achieve the
therapeutic goals. Since the short-term therapist depends on other
people in the child's life to do much of the therapeutic work, simple
precise communication is essential. By the information that is sharing
and by his language and demeanor, the therapist seeks to demystify the
treatment process. Efforts are continuously made to engage the parents
and teachers as colleagues in the treatment of the child and to respect
them as experts in their own right. In many cases, the role of the therapist
is intentionally down-played in order to focus the responsibility for
change on the significant adults in the child's life.

The communication begins with the written plan or therapeutic
contract that clearly states what the therapist expects to achieve and how
he expects to do it. The specifics of writing a therapeutic plan are
discussed in detail in Chapter 2.

The second level of interaction consists of an ongoing dialogue
in which the therapist methodically communicates with parents,
teachers, or other significant adults about their roles in the implementation of the therapy. This interaction is most intense and effective when it
is in the form of family therapy. Within the therapy session, the therapist
communicates on many different levels with the child's "system," providing opportunities for the family members to not only hear about how
they might change, but to actually experience it. Another form that this
interaction might take is when the therapist identifies a person in the
child's life to act as a "co-therapist" in the treatment. In this instance the
adult, usually a parent, is trained to carry out a therapeutic technique
that is part of the overall therapy plan. Co-therapists may be chosen not
only for their ability to implement the specific technique, but also for
their ability to restructure the child's family system.

The third level of interaction puts the therapist in a consultative
role. He/she may advise the teacher on specific techniques to help the
child in the classroom, or may provide information to the family on such
matters as the diet for a hyperactive child or how to listen to and talk to a
child who has suffered the death of a parent. The consultative role of the
therapist may involve a full range of therapeutic techniques. The teacher

who cannot provide limits for the child may be asked to come in for assertiveness training. The father who cannot control his anger may be invited to see the therapist for his own treatment.

The fourth level of communication is directed toward other professionals. The multidisciplinary approach will be familiar to most therapists who have worked in a hospital or school setting, but there is no reason why this same approach cannot also be used in a community setting with complex or difficult cases. A multidisciplinary approach draws selectively from a host of specialists including: speech/language therapists, pediatricians, pediatric neurologists, occupational therapists, creative arts therapists, specialized tutors, and so forth. The approach will include diagnostic assessments by each specialist, a plenary meeting to present the initial findings and draw up an interdisciplinary treatment methodology, and ongoing followup meetings to evaluate the progress being made.

Finally, therapists may be called upon to act as advocates for the child as part of the short-term therapy process. While this may be beyond what we usually refer to as "therapy," getting a child the appropriate educational, medical, or social services that he/she needs can sometimes be the most significant intervention therapists can make. To be effective advocates, therapists should familiarize themselves with federal and state laws regarding the rights and services available to children, and they should not hesitate to represent children before agencies who are delegated by law to serve them.

CONFIDENTIALITY AND INTRUSION

In trying to interact dynamically with children and their environment, we also create some difficult problems and questions about our roles as therapists. Two issues amplified by short-term therapy are the client's right to privacy about his/her treatment, and the intrusion, or disruption that the treatment causes in the life of your client.

The problem of confidentiality is usually of most concern to children in regards to their families. One child is afraid that the therapist will report to his parents that he has been stealing again. Another thinks that the therapist will spill the beans on how angry she is with her father, causing him to leave the home. A third thinks that the therapist will tell her parents about her sexual feelings towards her teacher. Every stage of childhood has its secrets, and every child must be assured that the therapist respects him or her. But sometimes the right to privacy is over-shadowed by the need for open and direct communication about the child's problems.

The general rule of thumb is that while thoughts and feelings are the sole province of the therapy room, a child's actions are often shared with other adults. It is sometimes surprising how easy it is for children, even very young ones, to comprehend this. Children are used to being talked about by people who care for them; it happens all the time with their parents, and they can accept this as a part of life. They do not necessarily distrust the therapist who also talks to their parents, as long as the therapist's intentions are made clear from the beginning of the treatment.

Any technique that disrupts the child's normal day-to-day life is an intrusion, but certain types of short-term therapies are inherently more intrusive than others. The general premise of short-term therapy is to minimize the disruption of a child's life by treating the problem as efficiently as possible, and the same rule of minimal intrusiveness applies in selecting specific techniques. But sometimes an intrusive therapy is unavoidable because of the crisis nature of the problem.

The issue of intrusion is a more common problem in the child's school than in his home. Children are very sensitive to their status with their peers, and having a "therapist" is rarely considered something to brag about. Even the children who seem to enjoy therapy and are deeply attached to their therapists are often embarrassed to be in therapy and do not want the therapist to visit their school and be seen by their friends.

The issue of intrusion in a child's life may manifest itself in subtle ways that the therapist must be attuned to. If a child is asked to wear a counter to record the frequency of some behavior, then the therapist must also realize that this will be observed by the other children in the class. If a teacher is asked to create a special work space for a child with a learning disability, then the therapist must consider how the child's status in the class will be affected and whether or not this intervention will do more harm than good. Any change in the child's life, no matter how appropriate it may seem to the therapist, can make him or her so self-conscious that the therapy will be undermined. Ideally, therapeutic interventions should be designed to have a maximum effect while being minimally intrusive, but realistically there appears to be an inverse relationship between the power of therapy to effect change and the disruption of the child's day to day life.

In some instances, such as problems that involve dangers to a child, the issue of intrusiveness must be put aside, and the most powerful techniques available should be used. In these circumstances, the therapist should know as precisely as possible when and how the behavior will change. For a further discussion of this issue, see Chapter 9 on on-site therapeutic techniques, the most intrusive of the interventions discussed in this book.

CONTRAINDICATIONS FOR SHORT-TERM THERAPY

For some children short-term therapy is not the treatment of choice. These children include ones who have not completed the bonding process that normally takes place between the parent and child in the first two years of life. Typically, they manifest severe personality disturbances such as autism, childhood schizophrenia, severe anxiety disorders, or chronic depression. What is most important for these children is to develop a relationship with an adult they can trust and care for, one who will meet them with nurturance and empathy. While this can certainly happen in short-term therapy, these children deserve to know the full benefit of complex and rich relationship with another human being without the limitations of time and expediency.

A second type of children for whom short-term therapy is contraindicated will have had at least a partially successful experience in bonding and will be proceeding along the road toward individuation. However, they remain vulnerable because they have had a substantial number of adult figures come in and out of their lives as a result of frequent moves, changes of teachers, and most commonly, divorce.

Unfortunately there is no hard and fast rule as to when short-term therapy might harm these children by presenting still another important person in their lives who comes and goes. Certainly many therapists treat children (and their families) for adjustment problems related to divorce or other types of loss in a relatively short time with effective results. But other times, brief therapy for these children has only a palliative effect, and their significant conflicts remain unresolved for many years, sometimes with irreversible psychic damage.

The only way I know to avoid the error of inappropriately treating these children with short-term techniques is to proceed with therapy only after a comprehensive diagnostic workup. In particular, the decision of whether or not to use short-term therapy on these children may rest on their ego development—how much they have formed an individuated sense of self; how they have developed a sense of their independency and mastery skills; the developmental stage of their peer relations; and, in particular, the structure of their ego-defense mechanisms. If, in fact, their developments have proceeded more or less along "normal" lines and if their personalities tend to be adaptive, then short-term therapy, focused on building support for the child within the family, might be indicated. However, if children have not successfully completed many of the appropriate developmental tasks expected at their ages, or they have had difficulty in meeting many of the demands and stresses of the maturational process, then long-term therapy would be indicated. In an open-ended, nondirective therapy, these children would have the opportunity to regress and return to unresolved issues which might be triggered by the immediate circumstances of their lives.

In some cases, the question of whether or not to use short- or long-term therapy has a simple solution—use both. On several occasions, I began using short-term therapy only to realize that a more intensive, longer treatment was needed. In these instances, the brief therapy became an extended period of diagnosis and helped determine important information about the exact kind of services that the child needed. In other instances, short-term therapists may work adjunctively with a child who is also in an open-ended long-term therapy. A short-term therapist might be used to implement a behavioral program for a specific problem in the home or school. Family therapy might be used to restructure the way that the parents respond to a child's chronic problem. Or dance/movement therapy might be used to stimulate preverbal or undifferentiated feelings into an adolescent's conscious awareness and so facilitate his progress in long-term, insight-oriented therapy.

A NOTE TO PARENTS

Although this book is primarily written for practitioners of psychotherapy or students, it may also be useful as a guide to parents in helping them choose a therapist for their child. Finding a therapist involves some of the most important and difficult decisions a parent must make and should be done with both caution and knowledge. There are several factors, however, that make this difficult process even harder. Parents are understandably in a hurry to get their children help. Usually things have gotten pretty bad before a professional is sought and the whole family feels a need for immediate relief. The parents may want to hand the problem over to the first therapist they meet, but this could be a big mistake.

Therapists are not all alike. They have many different views, theories, and practices, some of which will suit the child and the parents better than others. Sometimes any therapist will be able to help a particular child, but more likely this is not the case. Some will be better suited to the child's needs than others.

Another problem that parents face is the mystique surrounding psychotherapy, implying that the decisions about a child's treatment should be left up to experts. This attitude is misleading and potentially harmful. Parents are experts in their own right. They are the ones who have acknowledged their child's problems, and undoubtedly they will be part of the solution.

The informed opinion of experts should certainly be taken into consideration, but it can never supercede the responsibility of the parents to make the final decisions.

A third problem that parents face is where to look for a child psychotherapist. The child's pediatrician, the school principal, a clergyman, or a friend will often offer a name of a therapist, but I usually advise parents to consider at least three choices. If the parents cannot obtain three referrals through their own social network, then they can contact their local or state mental health agencies who maintain lists of both public and private therapists. Finally, there are national professional organizations that maintain lists of their credentialed members across the country, including the American Psychological Association, the American Psychiatric Association, and the National Association of Social Workers. All three organizations are located in Washington D.C.

Once the names of three therapists have been obtained, the therapists should be contacted by phone for an interview. Some therapists will charge for the first interview and others won't, and this should be ascertained in the initial phone contact.

During the interview the therapist will want to find out as much as possible about the child and his or her family, but parents should also use this time to find out about the therapist. Parents should feel free to ask whatever comes into their minds; however, these are some of the most important issues that I think should be pursued:

> What is the experience, orientation, and training of the therapist? How many children with similar problems has he or she seen, and what have been the outcomes?
>
> How often will the therapist see the child? Will other members of the family be present or be seen separately?
>
> How long might the therapy take?
>
> How will the therapist communicate with the parents? Does the therapist provide written reports, periodic meetings, regular phone calls? Is the therapist willing to visit the child's school if necessary?
>
> How will the therapist and the parents know if progress is being made? How will the success of the therapy be judged? Does the therapist provide a written contract which says what to expect and when?
>
> How much will the therapy cost? How are payments to be made? Does the therapist accept payments from insurance companies or other sources?

Most therapists will easily be able to answer these questions to the parent's satisfaction, for they involve issues that are a part of every therapeutic practice. But the parents should also pay attention to the way that they are answered: the responsiveness and warmth of the therapist, his or her voice tone, and patience, for these will give important clues as to how the therapist will interact with the child.

Although these suggestions are primarily directed at parents who are choosing a private therapist, many of them will also apply to therapists who might be assigned to a child either in a school or at a clinic. Most parents don't realize that these assignments are often made as much for practical reasons as for therapeutic ones, and that parents can, and should, have a voice in what will be a very important relationship for their child.

If you take your child to a public or private clinic for treatment, you will probably first be interviewed by an intake therapist who is responsible for assessing the problem and directing you to an appropriate treatment. This is the person who can answer the questions that I have just listed.

Often clinics will use students or trainees to treat a large proportion of their clients; however, the fact that a therapist is relatively inexperienced has advantages as well as drawbacks. Usually therapists in training make up in enthusiasm and energy what they may lack in expertise, and children can be particularly responsive to the excitement and sense of adventure these new therapists bring. Still, you should rightfully be interested in just how student therapists will be supervised, how often, in what format, and whom they are accountable to. If you are not happy with the answers to these questions, or with the therapists themselves, then you should make this known as soon as possible.

The main point to remember is that mental health personnel and systems are usually more flexible and more receptive to "consumers" then most people think. If you speak up, you are likely to be heard.

2

A Model for Implementation

The model I use to do short term therapy assumes that the most comprehensive approach to a problem is also the most direct one. Since the intent of brief therapy is to maximize the impact on the child's conflicts while minimizing the actual treatment time, the therapist may spend as much time conceptualizing the therapy as actually doing the treatment. This chapter will describe a six step process to implement short-term therapy, from the initial assessment of the child to post-treatment followup. As Figure 2.1 shows, this is a sequential model that is linked by ongoing data collection, which is determined by the initial assessment and in turn determines the character of the subsequent steps.

To many, this model for doing short-term therapy will not seem to be short at all. Traditional long-term therapists may leave out some, if not all, of these steps and yet still report consistent success. But we cannot forget that traditional therapists have the luxury of time which allows them to be more informal and in some ways less precise. Short-term therapy leaves little room for error. Therapists with only a limited amount of time to see a child must act forcefully and directly, and only the clear knowledge of their clients and the effectiveness of their techniques can allow them to do so.

Several times in this book I will mention the work of Milton Erickson, the undisputed grand master of brief therapy, whose recent death in 1980 has had a double-edged effect on the use of short-term techniques. On the one hand, renewed interest in Erickson's amazing style has opened the door to the creative use of nontraditional techniques. But on the other hand, those therapists who have tried to emulate Erickson's informal, seemingly intuitive methods may be doing a dis-

FIGURE 2.1. Model for Short-Term Therapy

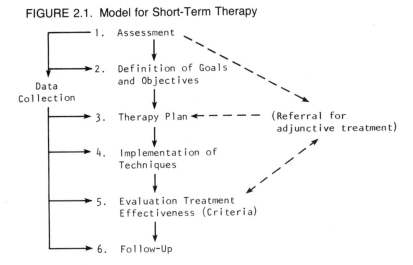

service to his genius, as well as to their patients. Anecdotes abound of Erickson's remarkable therapeutic successes, many of which took place with only a few hours of treatment. For instance, there is the case where Erickson treated a psychiatrist and his wife who flew 1,500 miles to be treated for three sessions. Although they each had been in psycho-analysis for years, they remained unhappy in their marriage and unful-filled in their careers. After a week, they returned home and in a six month followup conducted by Erickson, they reported that for the first time in their adult lives they were each making the kind of personal and job choices that brought them a sense of self-worth and fulfillment.

There was also the case of an eight year old boy, brought kicking and screaming into Erickson's office. His parents had sought help from their neighbors for their son's bedwetting, they had prayed publicly for him in church, and now, in desperation, they wished to take him to the "crazy doctor." Erickson effected a cure of this over-determined symptom in one short interview with the boy and one interview with the parents. An eighteen month followup indicated that the symptom had not returned, nor had another come to take its place. These are just a few examples of the hundreds of cases that Erickson treated in just a few sessions, at lectures with hundreds of people attending, by telephone and letter, even by proxy through another person, without ever making contact with the identified patient (see *Uncommon Therapy*, by Jay Haley, 1973).

It would be a mistake to think that because Erickson did not go through the formal conceptual steps that I am recommending his method was less systematic. Although he didn't use standard psychological testing, he was a brilliant diagnostician and his percep-tiveness was legendary. Although he didn't write formal therapy plans as I recommend, he practiced therapy in a time of less concern for professional accountability, and the stature he achieved in his years of clinical practice gave him a credibility that few of us will ever achieve. Erickson did not keep data on his clients, per se, but he was an avid and tireless researcher and developed many of his techniques through countless experiments and demonstrations. He was fortunate enough to practice in a city where he was an integral part of the medical, psychological, and social community, and his vast network of friends and professional acquaintances allowed him to follow up, both indi-rectly and directly, on an enormous number of his patients.

Perhaps some readers, like Erickson and other pioneering scien-tists, will be able to take shortcuts in the short-term therapy due to their years of experience and their exceptional talents. But for most of us, exacting methodology and articulate documentation must precede our art as the best guarantee of effective short-term therapy.

THE DIAGNOSTIC ASSESSMENT

Few therapists disagree on the importance of diagnostic assessments in child psychotherapy, but when it comes to designing therapeutic programs, hardly anyone pays attention to them. There are several reasons for this. The diagnostic assessment of a child is often done by someone other than the therapist. Diagnosticians are trained to describe with as unbiased an eye as possible the strengths and weaknesses of each child, but they may not be trained in psychotherapeutic techniques. While they may recommend therapy, they will usually be reluctant to indicate the exact extent and nature of what it should be, leaving the potential therapist with the job of doing additional diagnostic work. Besides not providing specific recommendations for the therapy, the information that they do provide may not be useful for writing the therapeutic plan. For instance, if the therapist has a behavioral orientation and the diagnostic profile does not include an adequate behavorial assessment of the referring problem, then the other information will be of little importance. Or if the therapist has an orientation toward reality therapy, which rejects the medical model of psychological disorders altogether, then even the most brilliant psychoanalytically oriented report will have little value.

A comprehensive diagnostic profile should do three things: make a differential diagnosis of the child's problems; specify hypotheses about the nature of the child based on the data; and provide detailed recommendations for treatment, including referrals or referral sources if appropriate.

The major classification system in use today has been provided by the American Psychiatric Association in their recently revised *Diagnostic and Statistical Manual III* (DSM-III). Although there is still some reluctance from the psychological community to use this system, there is also acknowledgement that the latest revision from the APA has addressed many of the complaints about its predecessor and may be a useful tool for differential diagnosis. In particular, the DSM-III has recognized the need for more than just a single word or phrase to describe a person's state of mental health. Instead, the DSM-III provides for diagnosis to occur on five axes:

> Axis I: Clinical syndromes; conditions, not attributable to a mental disorder, that are a focus of attention or treatment; additional codes.
> Axis II: Personality disorders; specific developmental disorders.
> Axis III: Physical disorders and conditions.
> Axis IV: Severity of psychosocial stressors.
> Axis V: Highest level of adaptive functioning in the past year.

The use of Axis III assures that the nonmedically oriented therapist will not neglect the consideration of relevant organic factors. The use of Axes IV and V focus the therapist on environmental and systems factors which might be important in the patient's treatment.

But determining a differential diagnosis is only the beginning of the assessment process. A thorough diagnostic profile must consider the child's intelligence, perceptual abilities, speech and language, neurological involvement, personality, academic success, behavior, family system, and social development. Whether or not this information is obtained from formal testing or informal procedures, the consideration of each of these factors will provide the therapist with the critical information needed to determine which therapeutic techniques will be most effective.

A treatment plan that uses multiple techniques will be most effective when each technique is systematically matched to the client's strengths, weaknesses, overt and underlying problems. But this is a formidable task. There is a scarcity of research to tell us which kind of therapies work with which children and because of methodological problems it is unlikely that such studies will be forthcoming. However, in spite of the fact that therapists will have few hard and fast rules to guide them, a systematic procedure for selecting therapies can still be developed. The Assessment Matrix (Figure 2.2) is an example of how the therapies covered in this book could be selected using a child's diagnostic profile as a guide. The Matrix consists of a list of 65 therapeutic constructs that could be considered in a comprehensive diagnostic work-up. These constructs, listed vertically on the matrix, are indexed to the fourteen major therapeutic techniques covered in this book. By comparing the strengths and weaknesses revealed in a child's diagnostic profile with the strengths and weaknesses that each technique addresses, you will have a general guide as to which therapies would be appropriate to use in a short-term treatment plan.

DIRECTIONS FOR USING THE ASSESSMENT MATRIX

Begin by considering whether each of the diagnostic factors listed on the vertical axis of the Matrix are relevant to the child's presenting problem. Then, in the first (and only empty) column indicate whether each factor represents a strength in the child's profile (by entering a blackened circle), a weakness (by entering an empty circle), or a combination of strengths and weaknesses (by entering a circle half black and half white). Any diagnostic factor that contributes to the child's overall maturation and adaptive growth could be considered a strength. A "weakness" might be a delay in the child's development, a fixation at a particular stage, or a maladaptive deviation from normative development. Other factors, such as family patterns or a child's interests, may be seen as having either a positive, negative, or mixed effect on the child's development. If a factor has no relevance to the child's treatment whatsoever, then no entry should be made.

Once this column has been completed, then match each circle that has been entered with the circles in the same row, putting a check through each circle that is the same (in other words, you are comparing the circle that you have entered with the fourteen circles in the same row). When you have done this for each of the 65 diagnostic factors, add the total number of checks you have made in each column and put this number in the boxes indicated "Total." The columns with the higher number of checks should indicate techniques that are particularly appropriate for use in a multimethod treatment plan for the child you are working with. To verify this, read the chapter describing each technique.

Remember that the Assessment Matrix is just a general guide, not a formula for the selection of techniques. The Matrix *does not* consider the factor of the age of the child nor does it weight any of the different constructs the way the therapist must do. The indicators and contraindicators for success listed in the beginning of each chapter should also be used as a guide in the selection of specific techniques, but your own therapeutic and diagnostic skills must be the final arbiter for the design of the therapy plan.

MEASURING THE PROGRESS OF THERAPY

The multi-method approach to treating the psychological problems of children assumes that our diagnostic techniques can only give us a general idea of the best treatment strategies for an individual child. We only find out what really works once therapy has begun; at that point we discard techniques that are less effective and make the ones that the child is responding to more precise. But we would still be stumbling in the dark if we didn't have objective methods of assessing the child's problems to show us the way. There are four basic methods to measure the progress of a child in therapy: direct, indirect, naturalistic, and self-monitoring. If possible, I prefer to use them all simultaneously.

The direct technique of measurement is the most empirical. This is a digital system of measurement which records what actually takes place, not what is inferred. Either something happens or it doesn't. This is the most quantifiable form of measurement and the one open to the greatest degree of statistical analysis. This type of measurement includes

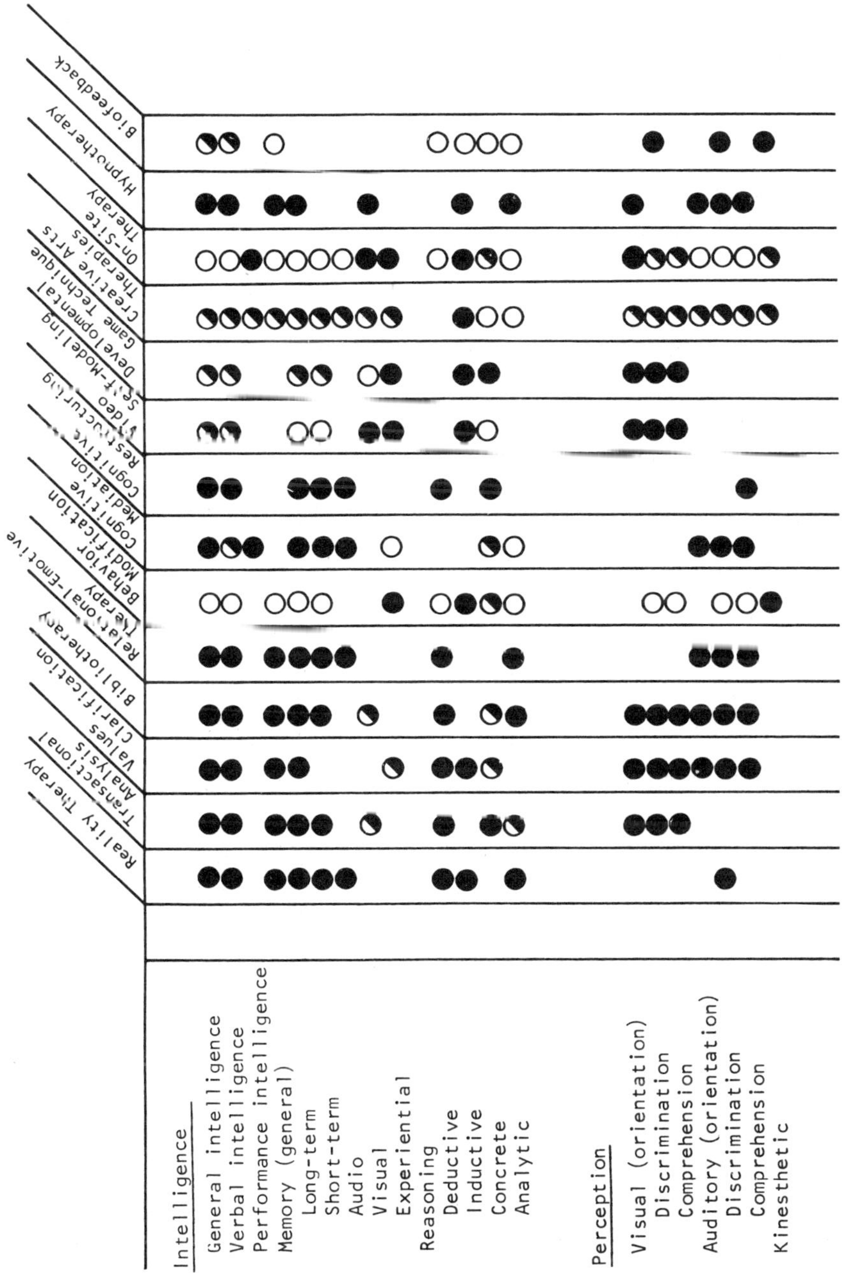

FIGURE 2.2. The Assessment Matrix

Matrix of therapies and presenting conditions.

Therapy	Language/Speech — Communication	Articulation	Language ability	Nonverbal	Academic — Underachievement	Overachievement	Attention span	Learning style	Study habits	Organization	Neurological — Retardation	Minimal brain damage	Organic syndromes	Physical handicaps	Gross motor	Fine motor	Personality — Reality testing	Emotional liability
Biofeedback																		
Hypnotherapy	○	○	○				○	○	○		○	○	○	○	○			
On-Site Therapies	●	●			○	○	○	○	○	○							●	○
Creative Arts Therapies	○	○	○	○	○		○	○	○	○	○	○	○	○			○	○
Game Technique	◐	○	◐	○	○	○	○	○	○	○	○	○	○	○	○	○	○	○
Developmental Self-Modeling	○	○	●	●	○		○	○	○	○	○	○	○	○	○	○	●	●
Video	○	○	○	○	○		○	○			○	○	○	○			○	○
Cognitive Restructuring	●		●				○	○	○								●	○
Meditation	◐		◐		○		○	○	○	○							●	●
Cognitive Behavior Modification	○	○	○	○	○	○	○	○	○	○	○	○	○	◐			○	○
Relational-Emotive Therapy	●		●				○	○									●	●
Bibliotherapy	◐		●	○	○	○	○										○	○
Values Clarification	◐	○	●		○	○		○					○				●	
Transactional Analysis	◐		◐										◐				○	○
Reality Therapy	●		●		●		●										●	

Personality (cont.)
- Object relations
- Ego development
- Ego defense mechanisms
- Mastery
- Autonomy
- Identity
- Ability to love and care
- Psychosexual development
- Extreme affective states

Behavior
- Habits
- Aggressiveness
- Withdrawal
- Impulsiveness
- Assertiveness
- Other problem behaviors
- Movement patterns

Family Structures
- Inappropriate role
- Differentiation of self
- Scapegoating
- Triangulation

Column headings (therapies):
Biofeedback · Hypnotherapy · On-Site Therapies · Creative Arts Therapies · Game Technique · Developmental Self-Modeling · Video Self-Modeling · Restructuring · Cognitive Meditation · Behavior Modification · Relational-Emotive Therapy · Bibliotherapy · Clarification Values · Transactional Analysis · Reality Therapy

Interpersonal Relations	Reality Therapy	Transactional Analysis	Values Clarification	Bibliotherapy	Rational-Emotive Therapy	Behavior Modification	Cognitive Mediation	Cognitive Restructuring	Video Self-Modeling	Game Development Technique	Creative Arts	On-Site Therapies	Hypnotherapy	Biofeedback
Peer relations	O	O	O	O	O	O	O	O	O	◐	O			
Relations with authority figures	O	O	O		O	O	O	O	O	O				
Play														
Competitiveness														
Cooperativeness		OOO			OOO	OOO		OOO	OOO	OOO				
Group participation	O						O							

Total number of checks in each column

a vast array of behavioral assessments, including direct observation, time sampling, analysis of videotaped sequences, and the measurement of physiological changes. Direct measurement techniques provide the therapist with the most up-to-date information about the way the child is changing, but they can also be very time consuming.

For this reason, care must be taken in choosing exactly what variable the therapist will measure. In every treatment, there will be several behaviors that will be changing, but the therapist must choose the one or two that will best reflect the child's developmental progress. For example, in measuring the progress of a child with an attention deficit disorder and hyperactivity, there are at least four variables that might be measured: overall activity level, length of attention span, ability to stay seated and work, and the amount of disruptive behaviors the child exhibits in school. Each variable would have specific implications for the treatment, and one would be more important in one child than in another. In addition, the importance of each variable would have to be weighed against the ease and practicality of the measurement itself.

Indirect measures are used for the assessment of hypothetical constructs which we assume to exist, but they cannot be observed or recorded by any of our senses. In indirect data collection techniques, we do not assume that there is a one-to-one correspondence between the event and the measurement, but rather that we are assessing a variable that may consist of a class of behaviors—attitudes, thoughts, or affective states. Standardized psychological tests are indirect measurement tools, which when defined in specific contexts, give us a meaningful, though intangible, construct. Nearly every type of therapy is built on hypothetical constructs, but the extent to which they are measurable will depend on the development of tools which have proven validity and reliability. Continuing our example, some of the constructs we might be interested in with a hyperactive child would include: self-esteem, impulsivity, style of problem-solving, and learning ability. Each of these can be measured by one or more standardized tests with varying degrees of efficiency and reliability.

Ideally, the therapist will choose psychological tests which have high validity and reliability coefficients and which have two forms for the same measurement, one for the pretest and one for the post-test. However, even when this is not the case, these tests can be used to get interesting qualitative data. Before selecting a test for a pre- and post-measure of change, the therapist should be familiar with how to statistically analyze the results, so that he or she won't be interpreting changes that are artifacts of the test.

Naturalistic measurements include all kinds of information that arc already available in the child's life (as opposed to data which is a by-product of the therapy). For a hyperactive child we would certainly want to keep track of changes in his height and growth, particularly if he were on any type of medication whose side effects included a slowing of the rate of growth. Grades are another measurement which exists in the child's "natural" environment and along with standardized achievement tests administered by the school system (usually in the first, third, and fifth grades), may be the most important indicator of change for this type of child. Usually by the end of puberty, overactivity and impulsiveness diminish in all children, but their lack of achievement in their early years of school can continue to be a lifelong handicap. For this reason I would pay relatively less attention to the question of whether or not a child is sitting and behaving himself, and put primary emphasis on the question: "Is he learning all that he can?"

Methods by which a child monitors his or her own progress are actually subsets of either direct, indirect, or naturalistic data collection, but are important enough to be considered in a category of their own. They are important because they contribute to the child's sense of control of his or her own life—an unquestionable therapeutic benefit no matter what the referring problem. Self-monitoring techniques can include a large range of measures, depending on the child's age, interests, and, of course, his/her ability to carry them out. As in selecting any intervention technique, self-monitoring measures should only be used when it is clear that the child will succeed in using them. For a hyperactive youngster, self-monitoring techniques could include: keeping track of the number of assignments he completes in a day by adding them up and plotting the numbers on a graph; keeping track of the number of times he raises his hand to ask a question, rather than calling out, by using a simple wrist counter; or keeping the records for a behavioral contract for the chores he does around the house. It is preferable to have a child measure an increase in his new, positive behaviors, rather than a decrease in the negative ones. Focusing on behaviors that you want the child to eliminate may also focus him on the slow rate of change or how much work is involved in giving up old habits and behaviors. This in turn may make the child feel that he has been really "bad," diminishing his self-image and thus defeating the purpose of using self-monitoring.

GOALS AND OBJECTIVES

A statement of the goal of the therapy and its breakdown into specific measurable objectives bridges the initial diagnostic assessment and the formal treatment. The goal is a restatement of the referring problem filtered through the hypothetical constructs revealed by the assessment. It should be stated in general terms, but not ambiguous ones. The goal(s) should be a statement of facts about what the therapy will do and will not do, and should be clear to the psychologically unsophisticated reader. While technical terms may be helpful in conceptualizing the diagnosis, they should be translated for the treatment plan.

The following examples are *not* acceptable statements of the goal of the therapy due to their lack of clarity:

- "The object of therapy is to alleviate Robert's symptoms and improve his self-concept." (What symptoms? What does the writer mean by "self-concept"?)
- "As a result of psychotherapy, Susan will become a more integrated young woman, and will be able to pursue her schoolwork with more drive." (What is an "integrated" person? How will her schoolwork actually improve?)
- "The following results can be expected as benefits from Jim's therapy: more differentiation among his family members; better ego-strength for Jim; a lessening of hostility and anger for Jim at school." (What kind of sense will Jim's parents make of this goal?)

Since the treatment plan will serve as a contract between the therapist and the parents, the goals of the short-term therapy should be stated in clear verifiable terms. Whether or not the therapy plan actually designates the use of any behavioral techniques, the goal will usually be stated in behavioral terms, for the way a child acts is the only thing that we can measure with any degree of certainty. While the therapist may be interested in subjective intrapsychic changes such as self-esteem, identity, mastery, and so forth, unless these can be operationally defined in verifiable terms, they should not be part of the therapy goal. But this caveat may not be as limiting as it sounds. Most intrapsychic concepts *can* be formulated in observable terms (this is how most psychological tests are constructed). Let's take the construct of self-concept as an example. How would you know when an adolescent is feeling better about herself? She might take more interest in her appearance. She would certainly make more positive statements about herself and fewer negative ones. She might go out with her friends more often. She might take more interest in her schoolwork and her grades would improve. All of these changes would be verifiable and could be legitimately stated as part of the goals of therapy.

The objectives of the therapy plan form the steps leading up to the main therapy goal. They define precisely just what changes will occur, under what circumstances, and to what degree. They should be carefully stated so that the technique to be used to achieve the change will logically follow. For example, an objective which predicts a cognitive change would be followed by a cognitive intervention strategy on the treatment plan, an anticipated change in the family would be followed by family therapy techniquess, etc.

The following goals and objectives were written for a 12-year-old who was diagnosed as an underachiever who had a mild school phobia. The psychological assessment revealed that his difficulty in school lay in part with his anxiety about being seen as a failure, which was almost assured because of his lack of study skills. Note how the statement of the goals tells the parents just what they can expect from the therapy.

> *Goals:* David will exhibit age-appropriate school work habits, including the ability to take a test, to do one-half hour of homework a night, to participate in group discussions, and to work independently in school as requested by his teachers.
>
> *Objective 1:* David will be able to work independently for half-hour periods at home and at school.
>
> *Objective 2:* David will demonstrate his ability to participate in group discussions by a) making a five-minute presentation to a small group, b) raising his hand to be called on at least twice in each discussion period, c) increasing his eye contact as he speaks and listens by 50%.
>
> *Objective 3:* David will complete two independent research assignments during the Spring term.

Here are other examples of goals and objectives for a ten-year-old boy referred for "classroom behavioral problems." Psychological testing revealed an immaturity in social relationships and in his identity formation, largely based on conflicts within the family, and manifested in the school because these conflicts couldn't be dealt with at home. Note how the statements of the goals and objectives can become a therapeutic intervention themselves, helping the parents to reframe their child's "school problem" as one which involves them as well. The language of the goals and objectives is meant to pave the way for the parents' acceptance of family therapy, without burdening them with blame for their son's problems.

> *Goal:* Peter will learn to see other people's point of view, including that of his parents, teachers, and peers. He will learn that there are ways to express his anger which are socially acceptable and which do not interfere with his school achievement.
>
> *Objective 1:* Peter will be able to identify and utilize six or more ways to express his feelings and opinions in appropriate ways at home and at school.
>
> *Objective 2:* Peter will develop listening skills, including paying atten-

tion to others when they speak, and reflecting back their literal and emotional messages.

Objective 3: Peter will exhibit more age-appropriate cooperative behaviors at home and school, including doing chores around the house and demonstrating 75% less disruptive behavior in school.

While it appears that these objectives are directed solely at changing Peter, in fact the therapy was also aimed at changing the way that Peter's parents, siblings, and teachers acted, as well. These objectives need not be explicit in the written plan, but may be implied. To state that a parent or teacher "must" change as part of the therapy would generally be counterproductive by putting these adults immediately on the defensive and stimulating both conscious and unconscious resistance.

WRITING THE THERAPY PLAN

Several years ago, I supervised a psychologist who had wonderfully creative ideas. He read vociferously and was always ahead of me in the latest techniques and issues. But when I reviewed his programs, most of which were to be carried out by parents and teachers, I could hardly keep awake past the introductory page. He wrote as if he were submitting an article to a journal, rather than trying to communicate a set of ideas and instructions to people whose only interest was to help a particular child. He used ten words when one would do and fancy terms when a common touch was needed. His writing was so full of jargon, catch-words, abbreviations and acronyms that I felt as though I were deciphering a code.

Above all else, a therapy plan should be written to be read. It should be in clear and simple English with a minimum of jargon or other kinds of psychological shorthand. The dictum to follow is: "make the reader want to read more."

Psychologists, and I include myself, have committed some of the worst crimes against language known to man. We are so concerned with the importance of what we say that we neglect to pay attention to the importance of how we say it. The use of jargon puts off the non-professional and is often misinterpreted by other professionals. It can be avoided much more than most of us like to admit. Acronyms and other abbreviations are handy for the typist, but they are an anathema to the reader. Wordiness is downright rude. Why punish the reader with extraneous words and murky phrases that the writer did not have the patience and resolution to make clear? Precision of language and thought is an invitation to the reader to share your wisdom.

At first, I thought that I would let the reports of my supervisee go unchallenged. He had worked so hard on them—fifteen to twenty pages for each one—how could I ask him for a rewrite? But no amount of

rationalizing could hide the fact that they were unreadable and unwork-
able as therapy plans. If I couldn't read them through, what could I
expect a parent to do? And if no one would read them, why write them in
the first place?

So I sent them back attached to a copy of Strunk and White's *The
Elements of Style.* I also included a list of writing hints:

1. Write in a way that comes naturally. Use words and phrases that come
   easily. Don't push. Don't try to impress.
2. Work from an outline or some other form of preparatory notes. One good
   outline is worth a dozen rewrites.
3. Emphasize the precision of your nouns and verbs. Adjectives and ad-
   verbs add color, but nouns and verbs carry the reader's attention and tell
   him what you want him to know.
4. Use the active rather than the passive voice.
5. Use concrete rather than abstract words.
6. Don't hesitate to rewrite. Thoughtful writing is always more efficient in
   the long run.
7. Avoid the use of qualifiers like "rather," "very," "little," "generally."
   Eliminate words that have no purpose. Spend words as if they each cost
   a buck.
8. Use plain and clear language.
9. Use good grammar.
10. Use figures of speech sparingly.
11. Employ a straightforward style that keeps the reader's interest, but
    doesn't keep him guessing.

Writing clear and readable treatment plans is not that difficult, but it
does take an initial investment of time to develop this skill, a commodity
in short supply to most therapists. On the other hand, once a therapist
develops an effective style and format for writing therapy plans, each
one becomes easier.

The format I use for a multi-technique therapy plan is designed
to be as amenable to change and revisions as the therapy itself. The first
page of the plan presents an overview of the program, consisting of seven
basic ingredients:

1. Basic identifying information and the introduction of the problem;
2. The goal of the therapy;
3. The behavioral objectives that will lead to accomplishing the goal;
4. The techniques to be used to achieve each objective;

6. The method of data collection that will be used to evaluate the progress
   of the treatment;
7. The criterion by which the success of the therapy will be measured.

Figure 2.3 shows an example of this form, where items 3 through 7 are combined in a chart to reference one another. A second form (see Figure 2.4) is repeated for each objective of the treatment plan. This form also doubles as an instruction page for parents or teachers who might be carrying out one or more of the interventions. Note that there are several places on this form to enter additions, revisions, or other comments, so

FIGURE 2.3. Treatment Plan

Client's Name: _____ Date of Initial Plan _____

       Address:_____

       Phone: _____ Name of Primary Therapist:_____

Parent/Guardian: _____ Address: _____

DSM III Diagnosis: Axis 1 _____ Phone: _____
               Axis 2 _____
               Axis 3 _____
               Axis 4 _____
               Axis 5 _____

Referring Problem:_____

Other Professionals Working with the Child: _____

Others' Involved in the Treatment Program: _____

Therapy Goal: _____

Objectives	Techniques to be Used	Principle(s) of Techniques	Method of Data Collection	Criteria for Succes
1.				
2.				
3.				
4.				
5.				
6.				

```
Page ____ of ____

Date _____


OBJECTIVE (#__):_____


Name of Technique:_____


Principle:_____


Description:_____
_____
_____
_____
_____



The technique should be implemented  (note revisions as applicable):
    Time/Events:_____
    Place: _____
    By: _____


Data to be Collected: _____


Revisions (note dates):_____
_____
_____
_____
_____
```

FIGURE 2.4. Techniques Form

that the treatment plan can be used to document changes as it becomes clear what makes each intervention most effective.

This format is also useful for cases involving several professionals from different disciplines. Each specialist is responsible for a Techniques Form describing what he or she is doing. As therapy progresses, each Techniques page is updated at regular interdisciplinary meetings, as each person presents his/her report on the child's progress. This revision system enables each person involved in the child's treatment to have constantly updated information, while eliminating the need for a constant river of professional reports.

The final page of the treatment plan, the Program Summary (see Figure 2.5), is added at the completion of the treatment. This page

FIGURE 2.5. Program Summary Form

Have the criteria for each of the objectives been met? Note reasons for success and/or problems:
Objective 1: _____
Objective 2: _____
Objective 3: _____
Objective 4: _____
Objective 5: _____
Objective 6: _____
Has the major goal of the treatment plan been met? Comment: _____
_____
_____

List the most important therapeutic principles culled from the Treatment Program:
1. _____
2. _____
3. _____
4. _____
5. _____
6. _____
Recommendations for maintaining therapeutic success: _____
_____

Other suggestions and/or referrals: _____
_____

Date for follow-up: _____
Method of follow-up: _____
_____

Post-treatment objective (optional): _____
_____
_____

indicates whether or not the criterion of each objective has been met, whether the criteria had to be changed, and whether or not any embellishments on the original treatment plan were made. Finally, there are recommendations of how the progress made in the formal therapy program can be maintained, and suggestions for other referrals, if appropriate. The date for the follow-up of the child's progress is noted and a new objective may be added to indicate what progress should be expected at that time.

THE CRITERION AND THE FOLLOW-UP

Since I am advocating a flexible and experimental approach to short-term therapy, how can therapists always predict precisely how the therapy will be concluded? The answer is that they can't. In setting the criterion for each objective, therapists can sometimes predict with precision, but other times they must endure a wide latitude in our not so exact science. Some techniques can have extremely predictable results, but these are also likely to be extremely intrusive and disruptive to the child's daily routine. Nevertheless, if the issue is important enough, the most powerful techniques should be employed and the criterion should be set rigidly. An example of an objective with an exacting criterion is: "Maude will decrease her head-banging from an average of 20 times per day to zero times per day within a period of 3 weeks." The need for a precise criterion to judge the effectiveness of the treatment here is obvious.

For objectives which may not be so critical to the child's immediate health or well-being, the criterion may be less precise and the estimate of success more conservative: "Joe will decrease the amount of times he teases his sister per week by 20 to 40 percent by the end of therapy."

Selecting the criterion is a skill that must be learned slowly after the experience of seeing many children with different problems and of developing a sense of the factors that determine the rate of responsiveness by different types of children to different techniques. With this in mind, we should not think of the criteria as written in stone; this should be made clear to parents, teachers, and others involved with the child's treatment. The criteria are guideposts, nothing more or less. If halfway through the treatment the child is not making any progress toward the predicted outcome, then every aspect of the treatment plan must be reevaluated. The specific objectives and criteria for success might be changed, new techniques might be added or old ones modified, or a complete reconceptualization of the therapy might take place, including the consideration of new or additional referrals. Careful documentation of this process in the treatment plan, however, will invariably lead the therapist towards the appropriate therapeutic strategies.

Whatever the final outcome of the therapy, following up on the progress of the child should be conducted at three- and six-month intervals. This is particularly important in brief therapy, since the formal program is often only the beginning of the change process for the child. Through the therapeutic interventions, the parents, the teacher, and the child have learned new ways to cope and deal with internal and external stresses, but they often need some reinforcement of continuing new habits and patterns. Anticipating a followup to the therapy will often be an incentive to continue doing the "therapeutic work." Sometimes the followup will reveal that additional consultation is needed due to changes in the child's life circumstances. Typically, in those cases, a few consultations will be enough to reorient the child's system so that it can continue to provide opportunities for the child to use his/her adaptive resources.

But the most important benefits of following up on cases may be to the therapists themselves. There is simply no other way to learn which techniques work in the long run and which ones do not. With each new case, therapists hone their talents and the effectiveness of their short-term models for treating children will grow.

3

Reality Therapy, Transactional Analysis, Values Clarification, Bibliotherapy, and Rational/Emotive Therapy

TYPES OF PROBLEMS

Adjustment Reactions of Childhood and Adolescence; Conduct Disorders; Delinquency; Improving Social Relationships/Peer Interaction; Parental Acceptance of Childhood Problems.

Indicators

The techniques described in this chapter are most appropriate for children who verbalize their thoughts and who are analytic in their thinking. They are particularly useful in the age ranges of 8 to 18. All the techniques in this chapter have been used with success in regular and special classrooms.

Contraindicators

These techniques would probably not be effective with children who are highly resistant to therapy, or who have verbal or cognitive deficits. While they may be used in a multiple-technique treatment program with children who have severe presenting symptoms, they should not be used in isolation in situations which call for immediate conflict resolution (e.g., school phobia, aggressiveness, self-abuse, etc.).

REALITY THERAPY: A RELATIONSHIP APPROACH

When William Glasser first introduced reality therapy in 1965, it was a radical departure from the traditional psychiatry practiced by his colleagues. With one sweep, Glasser rejected the entire concept of mental illness, simultaneously dismissing the need for the classification of emotional disorders. He rejected the idea of working with a patient's past problems to understand his present and claimed that exploring a patient's unconscious motivations served to excuse him from dealing with his present. He replaced the analytic stress on the significance of the transference phenomena with an emphasis on honest self-disclosure by the therapist, and broke the Freudian commandment of "thou shall not teach" by defining reality therapy as an educative process whereby patients learn to fulfill their own needs. Glasser (1965) sees all "patients" as suffering from an inability to fulfill two basic needs: "the need to love and be loved and to feel that we are worthwhile to ourselves." Helping people fulfill these needs is the essential focus of reality therapy.

      Glasser argues that these two needs are a constant among all humans, although we differ in our ability to fulfill them. Whether a person is a forty-year-old psychotic or a ten-year-old school under-achiever, the principles and techniques of reality therapy remain the same, since both these individuals suffer from having the same needs unfulfilled.

Glasser also maintains that in their unsuccessful attempt to fulfill their needs, all patients share the common characteristic of deny-ing reality. The girl who steals denies the warning of her parents that she will eventually be caught and punished. The adolescent who over-indulges in alcohol and drugs refuses to acknowledge the inevitable physical consequences that are inherent in the continued use of these chemicals and the fact that they have profound effects on his social relations, ability to perform, and even the way he thinks. Parents who deny that their marital problems have an effect on their children are likewise denying what they know about their own experiences as chil dren. At the same time, the people in these examples are demonstrating what Glasser calls "a lack of responsibility."

The concept of responsibility in reality therapy is defined as "the ability to fulfill one's needs and to do so in a way that does not deprive others of the ability to fulfill their needs." By this definition, each of the people we have described as denying reality can also be described as being irresponsible. By stealing, the child responds to her impulse for immediate gratification, but deprives the owner of the stolen object of his or her rights of possession. Although he may insist on his right to do with his body as he pleases, the adolescent drug abuser shows a lack of responsibility toward himself, his parents, and others. Parents who neglect the emotional needs of their children are irresponsibly raising children who will follow in their footsteps. The irresponsible person, argues Glasser, cannot possibly fulfill his or her needs for self-worth.

Parallel to his definition of human needs is Glasser's belief that reality therapy has two essential purposes: to teach the person how to care and be cared about through the example of the therapeutic relation-ship, and to teach people to be more responsible and more realistic.

The task of getting involved in an emotional relationship with the patient is essential to reality therapy. The therapist must be empathe-tic and sensitive to the patient, making it clear that he is totally invested in the relationship. But he must also be strong, even tough. He must have the strength to have his own values tested, to withstand severe criticism, to not be frightened or put off by the behavior of the patient no matter how eccentric, and be able to bare his own vulnerability and humanness without being caught up in the patient's suffering. The teaching of responsibility happens through the therapeutic relationship rather than through any didactic or advisory process. Glasser notes it is useless to discuss the patient's irresponsibility, for this would only encourage stubborn patients to justify their behavior. It is enough to jointly recognize that the patient's irresponsible behavior exists and that the patient is the only one who can do something about it. What should be talked about is the patient's present life—his or her interests, feelings, opinions, and, in particular, values. Talking about the patient's problems may be the least fruitful line of discussion. It is made clear that the therapist knows the patient will change if and when he/she is ready, and there is nothing that the therapist can say or do that will make the change come any sooner.

There are at least three benefits of presenting therapy as an open dialogue within a relationship rather than as a problem-solving process. First, it expands the horizons and awareness of patients beyond their immediate difficulties. While other therapies define their patients in terms of their symptoms or problems, reality therapy defines them as people, with many day-to-day experiences beyond the immediate concerns that brought them into treatment. Second, by hearing the therapist talk about many subjects, patients are presented with innumerable opportunities to test out the therapist's responsible attitude towards life and to find out if they are really involved with a responsible therapist. And finally, as patients become convinced that they are in a caring relationship with a trustworthy and reliable person, the therapist can relate the discussions to what the patients are presently doing with their lives, confronting them with the reality of what they do as compared to the reality of what they say.

If used as a single technique, reality therapy would be incompatible with many of the principles I feel are important in short-term therapy. It rejects the idea of differential diagnosis, favors a non-directive over a directive approach, does not take into account developmental differences in children, and focuses on individual responsibility rather than seeing the problems of children as derivatives of the system they live in. Nonetheless, if used as a part of a multi-method approach, the stress on responsibility in the therapist/client relationship as conceptualized in reality therapy can have important therapeutic benefits for certain clients.

The major part of Glasser's theory was developed in the early sixties at Ventura School, a treatment center for seriously delinquent adolescent girls. Glasser's success at Ventura, and I believe the relevance of his theories to antisocial adolescents in general, derives from the potent combination of creating a supportive caring environment with very specific limits and consequences for "irresponsible behavior." The open and honest relationship between the therapist and the patient may be the only realistic therapeutic stance with rebellious teenagers. Invariably they have had more than enough exposure to authority figures who are either self-righteous and condescending or self-consciously inhibited.

Although short-term therapy is by its nature directive, the therapist can still emphasize that it is the responsibility of the adolescent alone to change or not change as he or she wishes. The therapist presents strategies which the adolescent can choose from or reject altogether. The consequences of the adolescent's behavior remain as a reality factor whichever route is chosen.

Take for example the case of Paul, a fifteen-year-old described to me as "uncontrollable" by his mother, a single parent. Although a very likeable young man, Paul had managed to break nearly every rule that was imposed on him by his mother and his school. He drank, smoked pot, skipped school, didn't study, drove without a license, and stole from department stores. What was almost as amazing as the number of rules he found to break, was that he always got caught. Since his I.Q. was in the superior range, I assumed that he could have gotten away with much more than he did, but he seemed to enjoy the drama of being found out more than he enjoyed getting away with something. If nothing else, every time he was caught he had more rules and restrictions that he could break imposed on him.

When I began seeing Paul, his mother was desperate. Her health was suffering, she was in danger of losing her job, and she admitted to acting more and more irrationally with Paul. She made it clear that if things didn't improve soon with Paul, she would be forced to send him to a military academy that was known for its strict disciplinary code for incorrigible young men. At my first meeting with Paul, I told him that I had contracted with his mother to see him for fifteen sessions, in which time I thought I could help him improve his behavior. Specifically, I told him that he would have to cut out drugs, stop drinking until he was of age, go to school on time and stay there, and leave the "gang" with whom he most often got into trouble. I told him that I hoped he would change his attitude towards studying, since he was so bright and could probably do very well in school, but whether or not he applied himself to his studies was entirely his own affair.

I then went on to list the ways I thought I could help him—the multiple techniques of the therapy plan. The techniques included family therapy sessions, a behavioral contract with his mother, and the video self-modeling technique (see Chapter 6). I also listed other techniques and suggestions that I thought might be appropriate, but that I would leave in reserve until I got to know him better. With this done, I told Paul that I wanted to put "all my cards on the table." As much as I wanted to help him and his mother, I couldn't do anything by myself. If he wanted to change, then I thought that I could show him how. He would only have to indicate when he was interested. However, if he did not want to change, then I would respect his decision. He should know, though, that I agreed with his mother that things could not go on the way they were. He had a right to live his own life, responsibly or not, but not to drive his mother crazy. If he did not meet my criteria by the end of our fifteen sessions, then his mother would send him to military school at once.

It is important to note that I was emotionally prepared to do just what I said. Although I knew that Paul would suffer at the military school his mother had chosen, I knew that he would suffer far more if he were allowed to continue acting as he had. I harbored no pretensions that I could do anything for Paul that he would not do for himself, nor had I made any indications to Paul's mother that I could change her son's behavior without his cooperation.

Paul looked at me with astonishment when I defined the boundaries of our time together. He told me that he hated the idea of going to military school and would do anything he could to avoid it, but that he didn't know if he could really change that much in fifteen weeks. He wanted to know if he could see me twice a week and I told him that I would check with his mother, but that it was all right with me. Our adventure had begun. Paul's therapy lasted four months and included several sessions with his extended family. In a follow-up call six months later, Paul reported that he was getting all "B's" in school, that he had a new set of friends, and that he and his mother had a "working relationship."

Reality therapy has been used in many school systems because of its emphasis on humanism and the educative approach to mental health. As a preventive tool, the principles of reality therapy are taught to teachers, counselors, school psychologists, and even school administrators. As in individual therapy, the stress is on developing close human contact between teachers and their students and creating a classroom atmosphere which stresses moral values. It can also be effective when used as part of a milieu approach for classes of children with emotional and behavioral problems. The principles of reality therapy are particularly useful in defining the relationship between a teacher and her pupils and are readily compatible with other techniques mentioned in this chapter.

TRANSACTIONAL ANALYSIS (T.A.)

I have always been a snob about transactional analysis, and at least once this caused me to make a serious strategic error in treatment. Finding the language of transactional analysis to be offensive—too cute, highly jargonized, pretentious in its oversimplifications—I rejected it as a legitimate mode of treatment, in spite of the fact that hundreds of dedicated men and women have successfully treated children and adults with these techniques. The particular instance that helped me overcome my short-sightedness occurred when I was teaching psychology and working as a counselor at a school for emotionally disturbed adolescents in New York City. The school at that time (the early 1970s) operated entirely on psychoanalytic principles, and being enrolled in analytic training, as well as being analyzed, I was not exactly open to the newer techniques sweeping across the nation from the West Coast. So much for my excuses. There was a young man in our school, John, whom no one seemed to be able to get close to, and indeed this was the focus of his problem. I had him in my psychology class for two semesters and found him to be extremely bright, an obsessive learner, but deliberately antagonistic in all our interactions. One day he came into school, ran up to me in the entrance hall, and announced that he had "found himself" with transactional analysis. He immediately began talking to me in T.A. language, which I had heard before but didn't understand, and I made little attempt to hide my disinterest. John asked if we could read one of Eric Berne's (the founder of T.A.) books as a supplementary text in my course, and I replied that it was fine if he wanted to read and report on one as a special project, but that the school operated on a small budget and all the texts for the semester were already ordered.

In short, John was approaching me with excitement and enthusiasm about finding out something about himself—probably the first time he had done this in years—and I was turning him off like a spigot of hot water, due to my own prejudice and intellectual elitism. As I recall, John did find other people to talk with him about T.A. and stuck with it for the rest of the year until he graduated, but any progress he made learning to get closer to people and being accepted for himself was not augmented by my attitude or behavior.

Currently in my clinical practice I don't often choose transactional analysis as a mode of treatment, and find keeping up with its developments a chore. However I recognize that this system of thinking about people and their relationships can be very valuable.

Briefly, I'll review some of the core concepts in T.A. Transactional analysis is a humanistically oriented therapy, emphasizing the right and ability of each individual to develop his/her potential to be fulfilled, loving, and loved. The key phrase, popularized in the title of a book by Thomas Harris (1969), is that everyone is "O.K." Being "O.K." translates as having self-worth and an acceptance of one's strengths and weaknesses, values, and feelings. Transactional analysis asserts that we are all born O.K., but early on in life, we learn that certain things we do, think, and feel do not please the people who are most important to us, and their reactions make us feel not O.K.—childish, stupid, inferior. The conflicting messages we get from our parents and other people important in our growing years cause us to develop three distinct ego-states, or voices inside us: a child, an adult, and a parent. The child is the part of us that wants immediate gratification. It is the part of us that is selfish, demanding, inconsiderate, irrational, but also the part that can have fun and be creative. The parent voice inside us includes our beliefs, values, and prejudices. The parental voice often makes us feel badly about ourselves, telling us that we have misbehaved or not accomplished what we should. It also keeps tabs on our ethics and moral code and limits some of our excesses. The adult ego-state is the voice of rationality. It deals with the present by seeing the world as it is, not the way it should be. T.A. also recognizes subdivisions of these three ego states (such as the critical parent and the nurturing parent) and various ways that they can overlap.

Transactions in this schema occur in the form of "strokes" which can be physical or verbal or gestural. Positive strokes (called "warm fuzzies") are naturally what we all seek and like, but in their absence, negative strokes ("cold pricklies") will sometimes have to do. Anything is better than the absence of strokes, or human interaction.

There are many more interesting and useful concepts in T.A., but these are the basics. If you are new to transactional analysis, you might be interested in the *T.A. Primer* by Adelaid Bry (1973), which presents these same concepts with simple prose and illustrations. If you work with adolescents, where I think T.A. is particularly helpful, I would highly recommend the book *T.A. for Teens* by Alvyn M. Freed (1976), Dr. Freed has also written books for younger children (*T.A. for Kids* and *T.A. for Tots*) and has developed records and audio-visual packages as well. There are perhaps more books written on the applications of T.A. than any other of the new psychotherapies. Many of these are published by Jalmar Press, Inc., 6501 Elvas Avenue, Sacramento, California 95819. Research on transactional analysis can be found in the "Journal of Transactional Analysis" found at many university libraries.

A successful use of transactional analysis occurred in the treatment of Janet, a seventeen-year-old with a severe behavioral problem at home. In the office Janet was shy and diffident, as well as slightly coquettish, and it was difficult to imagine her as the defiant shrew described by both of her parents. The therapy plan written for Janet included family therapy sessions to address her rebelliousness at home, but I also contracted with her and her parents to see Janet for ten individual sessions to help her with her "social problems at school."

Janet was extremely unhappy because she didn't have a boyfriend. She dated frequently, largely due to her seductive behavior with men that she had just met. But once they went out with her, the young men she flirted with wouldn't see her again. Often they responded to her forthright physical advances with immediate sexual overtures, and then when she became coy and old-fashionedly romantic, they quickly left the scene. With each new experience, Janet found herself hopelessly in love, and pined unhappily until the next prospective "boyfriend" came along. The idea of using T.A. with Janet first occurred to me when I saw her doodling in the waiting room before one of our appointments. Her drawings, which were original and very creative, were a concretization of her romantic daydreams and dating experiences. They were drawn in a comic-book style, each one telling a similar story of unrequited love and frustrated passion. The dialogue was extremely melodramatic:

JOSÉ: "My darling. I will never see you again. I go off to fight a battle I could never win. I will probably die, but I shall have your name on my last whisper.
EDWINA: Oh, José, my darling, I will never forget you. Give me your ring and I will wear it next to my heart until they bury me."

The next session I began to talk to Janet about the principles of trans-actional analysis, using illustrations to talk about the three different voices in all of us, how to give strokes, and so on. My illustrations were laughable compared to Janet's and for her homework, I had Janet draw me her own examples of what she had learned. As I had hoped, her examples were about dating. She drew a cartoon story about a boy who ran after girls because the "child" inside him kept seeking positive strokes by getting attention from girls. But when it came to having a deeper relationship with a girl, the "parent" voice inside him gave out only prohibitions: "If you get involved you'll only get hurt. You'll get someone pregnant. You'll get a disease."

We then began to role-play Janet's own dating experiences from her initial encounters with a new boy to her depression about being rejected. After each scene we drew cartoons of how a conversation might look if her "adult" voice was talking to the "adult" voice of her date. About five sessions later, Janet was fixed up with a boy from out of town. It was the first date that she could remember where she had not first "thrown herself" at the boy to get him to ask her out. Using T.A. diagrams, we conjured up what their transactions might be if Janet acted the way she usually did on dates, and then how they might look if she treated this new young man as one adult to another (see Figure 3.1). The date went off smoothly, and Janet continued to correspond with this young man until the end of our sessions together. In the remainder of our sessions Janet began to apply her new T.A. skills to other kinds of social

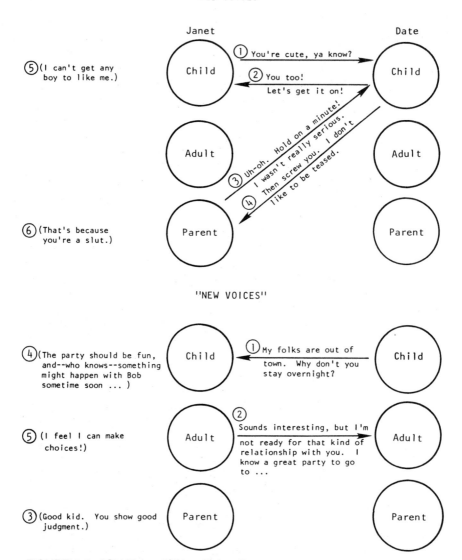

FIGURE 3.1. "Old Voices"/"New Voices"

relationships with her friends, parents, teachers, and, of course, with me. She read several of the books on T.A. and soon began to know much more about this method of self-analysis than I. In a letter I received from her after a six-month followup request, Janet told me that she was still dating the same boy from out of town, and had two other local boys whom she dated as well. She was graduating from high school that spring, and wrote that she was thinking of majoring in psychiatry . . . or bio-chemistry. She made it very clear that she saw her life as full of choices. And that she was feeling very "O.K."

VALUES CLARIFICATION AND BIBLIOTHERAPY

THERAPIST: So tell me about yourself. I'd like to get to know who you are. What do you like? What don't you like? What are your hobbies?

MARY: (AGE 8) Dunno, really. You know my name don't you? You know where I live. That's about it, I guess.

THERAPIST: Well, names and addresses are important, but they don't really tell me who you are inside. They don't tell me what kind of person you are.

MARY: I'm nobody special. Just somebody.

THERAPIST: Well, let's start with the basics. What do you like to do best in the whole world?

MARY: Watch T.V.

THERAPIST: Yes? What's your favorite show?

MARY: Oh, just about anything. I don't have any real favorites.

THERAPIST: And what is the second best way you like to spend your time?

MARY: Nuthin' really. Mommy thinks I like to do stuff like horseback riding, and swimming and stuff like that. But I don't really like it. It's pretty dumb. I just do those things to make her happy.

This bit of conversation was taken from an initial interview with Mary, a sad young girl whose parents had recently been divorced. Mary was one of the few children I have seen who was not defined by others as a problem. Her teacher said that she was a "good little student." Her mother said that she was a "good little girl." When I called her father in to get his viewpoint, he described Mary as a "trooper." He explained, "She's really taking all this right in her stride. She's going to be just fine. I wish that I could adapt so well!"

In fact, Mary was suffering from the divorce of her parents and not allowing herself to feel it. There was too much pain and no one around who could help her with it. To cut off the pain, Mary cut herself off from the rest of her feelings as well. As the preceding dialogue suggested, and as diagnostic testing confirmed, Mary felt empty inside. She had almost no feeling of self-worth or self-importance, almost no sense of self. Without therapy, Mary might at best continue to be mildly depressed for the remainder of her childhood. Her lack of interest in people might prevent her from attempting many developmental social tasks, predisposing her to a life of disappointing relationships. Perhaps she would look to the world of ideas to fulfill needs that were not met in the world of people, and would continue being a "good girl in school." But it is just as likely that her low-risk style would generalize to her academic work and she would achieve far below her potential. At worst, Mary's depression could become more ingrained and more serious. It could make her particularly vulnerable to many of life's stresses and turn into a chronic debilitating disorder. If the people in Mary's life continued to discourage her from feeling her own emotions, her personality defenses would become rigid and brittle and severe adolescent disorders would be possible.

Although she couldn't put her finger on just what was wrong, Mary's mother felt that Mary should be seen by a therapist. As discussed in Chapter 1 cases such as Mary's may not be appropriate for short-term therapy, but I agreed to see her for six months with the option of ongoing therapy to be based on a specific diagnostic criteria. As part of Mary's treatment, I used the closely related techniques of values clarification and bibliotherapy to encourage her to explore all her feelings, not only her parents' divorce, but every aspect of her life.

Values clarification, whether used as part of an individual treatment program or as part of a classroom's affective curriculum, consists of a series of exercises designed to encourage children to explore who they are. Rath et al (1966) suggest, the valuing process is composed of seven sub-processes, including prizing and cherishing one's beliefs and behaviors; publicly affirming this pride in appropriate forums; learning to choose from alternatives based on one's beliefs and behaviors; considering the consequences of each alternative; learning to choose freely; learning to act on one's values; and integrating one's values, choices, and actions into a consistent pattern.

There are many books of values clarification techniques such as Simon and Howe's classic *Values Clarification in the Schools* (1968). A sampling of these activities include:

> *Rating Scales:* Rate how you feel about the following things from 1 to 10: Dogs. People getting angry at you. Ice cream.
>
> *Forced Choice Exercises:* If you were on a desert island and could take only three people and three objects with you, what would you choose?
>
> *Diagrams and Charts to Explore Relationships:* Family tree collages, sociograms, etc.
>
> *Self-Concept Projects:* Design and build a model car that expresses five things about your interests.
>
> *Exploring Beliefs and Attitudes:* Role playing.
>
> *Interpersonal Exchanges:* Can you make a collage for your best friend showing everything you like about him?
>
> *Community Projects:* Since you believe that having a clean environment is so important, what can you do about it? List 10 projects that would help improve your neighborhood's ecology, and pick the one or two that you think you would like to do!

These are just a few of the infinite number of techniques that can be used.

While many values clarification books and kits on the market propose a systematic, step-by-step method of learning to value oneself, the luxury of individual therapy includes choosing the precise technique that will have the desired impact on a child. As in choosing any other technique in this book, the therapist must consider as many diagnostic factors as possible, including the child's developmental levels, ego-defense system, preferred sensory mode, interests, hobbies, and so on.

One of the first techniques I chose to do with Mary was to make a "Me Box." Mary had brought some small dolls with her to one therapy session, and when I asked her where she kept them at home, she replied, "They don't have any home in my home. I wish they did." From this wish, one of the first expressions of feeling that I had from Mary, we decided to make a special box to be a home for her dolls. The box would be decorated with pictures of things that Mary, or her dolls, especially liked. I asked her to sit down with her mother when she got home to pick out magazine pictures, photographs, her own drawings . . . anything that could be cut out, and bring the material with her to therapy the next week inside a shoe box.

She returned the next week with a box loaded with pictures and photographs. We then went through them, cutting out the ones that she liked, and we pasted these onto the box. Significantly, Mary had included several pictures of herself with her Dad, the first time she had mentioned him in therapy. She also had pictures of horses, children playing, ice cream . . . a more varied assortment than I would have predicted from our first interview together. As we pasted the pictures on the box, discussing them together, Mary commented on her mother's reaction to helping her pick out the pictures. "She cried a lot," Mary said, "about my Dad." And then she went on, "and I cried some, too."

As this example suggests, values clarification techniques can be effective because they are so simple and nonthreatening. While opening up a channel to the child's feelings, attitudes, and beliefs, they also enrich the relationship between the therapist and the child, or any other person involved in the therapy. When a parent is asked to participate in a values clarification exercise, it is almost inevitable that they too will be affected by its intent, and have their sensitivity and vulnerability aroused.

Bibliotherapy is exactly what the name implies: therapy through reading books. Since Dr. Spock's first book on child-rearing influenced a generation of children, hundreds of books have been written to help parents deal with the problems of children. More recently authors have also discovered the rewards of writing directly to an audience of children for therapeutic purposes.

While there have been many case histories of children who have been profoundly influenced by their reading, we still know relatively little about how to use this technique so that it is maximally effective for a particular child with a specific problem. What books will give the right "message" to the child? How can you know how the message will be interpreted? And even if the message is meaningful to the child, will it be translated into a new behavior, belief, attitude, or feeling?

As is the case with many therapeutic techniques, it is easier to identify children for whom bibliotherapy would not be an effective form of treatment, than children for whom it would be recommended. Obviously, children with reading difficulties or a poor attitude toward school would be less likely to get therapeutic benefits from a book; and children with poor abstract reasoning abilities or a highly egocentric point of view would have difficulty in applying the information or message from a book to their own lives.

To determine which children would be more likely to derive benefit from the bibliotherapy technique, we should look at the types of books that are being written for children:

> Books with a moral;
> Books about feelings;
> Books about coping;
> Books that give children facts or advice about common childhood concerns;
> Homemade books.

• *Books with a moral.* Going back at least to the time of *Aesop's Fables*, stories have been written for children to teach them a moral or lesson. This is still a popular genre of children's books although the contemporary fables are generally more subtle in providing a moral. Often animals or mythological figures are used to represent archetypal figures. The sly and witty fox, the evil witch, the virtuous prince and princess are a few examples.

• *Books about feelings.* These books usually tell a realistic story with children as the main characters. The stories are about everyday occurrences, such as friendship, death, moving to a new neighborhood, etc. They are aimed at helping children understand that emotions are a part of all our lives and need not be hidden.

• *Books about coping.* These books also stress that emotions are a normal part of life, but in addition they present story lines where the common conflicts of childhood are successfully overcome by the main characters. A boy who gets glasses learns to deal with being teased. A girl who has to go to the hospital learns that many of her fears are unfounded. A boy whose parents are paying more attention to a baby sister discovers appropriate ways to get attention for himself. It is assumed that by reading these books children will see alternatives to their maladaptive behaviors and will model the successful coping strategies of the characters in the book.

- *Books that give children facts or advice about common childhood concerns.* There are many books being published for children about subjects which parents have a hard time talking about. Richard Gardner's *Boys and Girls Book about Divorce* (1970) is an excellent example of this genre.

- *Homemade Books.* If you can't find the precise book that you want, you can always write one yourself. If you are like me and not much of an illustrator, then you can use magazine cut-outs, photographs, or very simple line drawings for the illustrations. You would be surprised how much "personality" a square, a circle, and a line can have when combined with a clever story line.

Most children find that stories with characters they can identify with are the most meaningful to them, and those with abstract morals least helpful. A major part of bibliotherapy is the interactive discussion with parents, teachers, or other children that these stories stimulate.

My own preference is for educative books that either provide important facts for children or present to them a realistic view of the world. As we shall see in the next section of this chapter on rational/emotive techniques, besides having their own egocentric viewpoints, children often learn irrational beliefs from their parents who give them information based on how reality *should* be. Books can help clarify the way things are.

Mary's parents' divorce was for the most part worked out in friendship, although both spouses suffered from recurring periods of guilt, remorse, and depression. But they didn't discuss any of this with Mary until the week before her father moved out. Finally, when a court date was set for the divorce decree, both parents sat down with Mary and asked her if she knew what a "divorce" meant. Mary replied that she had friends at school whose parents were divorced and that it meant that their mommies and daddies weren't going to be married anymore and that they weren't going to live together. Mary's parents agreed that this was exactly what they were doing. They told her that they were still going to be friends with each other, that they both loved her very much, and that she would still have two parents who just wouldn't be married. Afterwards, they congratulated each other on having raised such a "sensible" child.

Mary's parents didn't realize, as many parents don't, that her lack of questioning and apparent acceptance of their separation was based on her fears and wishes rather than on an accurate assessment of reality.

After about seven weeks of seeing Mary, we began to focus on her feelings about her parents' divorce, but they were very difficult for her to articulate. I didn't want to put myself in the role of a lecturer or educator, since she was just beginning to accept me as someone who could relate to her on her own level, so I asked her if she would like to read a book by Dr. Richard Gardner (The Boys and Girls Book About Divorce, 1970), who was someone who talked to children about their problems as I did, and who wrote a book just for children whose parents had gotten a divorce. She was immediately interested in the illustrations and seemed pleased to think that someone had written a book for children who were like her. I told her that I would be glad to give her a copy of the book, and said that she could read any part of it that interested her by looking at the Table of Contents and turning to that section (this is how Dr. Gardner suggests that the book be used in his Foreword). Some of the sections that caught her attention were: "How to Get Along Better With Your Divorced Father" and the "Fear of Being Left Alone." I also told Mary that I had a book to give to her mother, also by Dr. Gardner, called The Parent's Book About Divorce (1977), which might answer some of the questions that I thought her mother was having. Mary agreed that it would be nice for her mother to have such a book, sympathetically explaining, "she still seems awfully sad to me." I encouraged both the mother and daughter to talk about what they read with each other and with Mary's father if they wished. I also mentioned that I would like to hear their reactions to the book next week, if they chose to share them with me. As I had hoped, Mary reported in the following weeks that she had read most of the book I had given her, and had talked about what she read with her mother and father. Mary's father also borrowed both books and scheduled a separate session with me to talk about his feelings and reactions.

Learning to deal with reality while maintaining a sense of self-worth are some of the most important benefits of psychotherapy. If books can dispel myths, provide useful information, and stimulate shared feelings, then they can be an effective technique in many therapeutic programs.

RATIONAL/EMOTIVE THERAPY

Rational/emotive therapy shares a common principle with transactional analysis, values clarification, reality therapy, and bibliotherapy techniques: people obtain self-worth if they see themselves and their world as it *is* rather than distorted by fantasies and expectations of how they would like things to be. Albert Ellis, the creator of rational/emotive therapy, has written and lectured extensively about his techniques for more than twenty years, influencing many other psychological theories. While rational/emotive techniques have been applied for many years in working with children, particularly as an effective curriculum used in the classroom (see Knauss, 1974), my own preference has been to use Ellis's theory and techniques in working with parents to develop more realistic attitudes and behaviors toward their children, their spouses, and themselves.

Rational/emotive theory focuses on helping people give up their irrational belief systems and the consequent irrational self-defeating feelings and behaviors. Irrational beliefs are grounded in rigid, perfectionistic expectations of ourselves and others, which have little or nothing to do with the human condition. In addition, there is a belief that there is an order, predictability, and fairness in the "world" which exists simply because we wish it so. Irrational beliefs can almost always be identified by the absolute language used in stating these beliefs, and they can be recognized by the stated or implied use of "shoulds," "ought to's" and "musts." For example, let's take a father who has a boy who is school phobic. The parent thinks: "My son *should* not be fearful, it is not manly. I *must* do something to make him change. I *can't* have people think of me as a failure as a parent. *No one must* know that this problem exists." Each one of these beliefs is irrational. The boy *is* fearful. The father may be able to do something to help the child, but on the other hand, he may not. He has no way of controlling what other people think of him as a father, nor can he prevent people from finding out about his son's problems. Such irrational beliefs make the father feel ashamed, guilty, inferior, and fearful himself. If he clings to these irrational attitudes, his actions will reflect his desire to deny that the problem exists, making his son all the more confused.

Like the cognitive-behavior modification theorists whom he has greatly influenced (see Chapter 5), Ellis believes that if you change irrational ideas or self-statements, you will also change the feelings of despair, and powerlessness that are associated with them, along with the maladaptive behaviors that perpetuate the problem.

The first step in changing an irrational belief system is to identify which beliefs are based on observable data from the real world and which ones are based on perfectionistic, absolutist wishes and fantasies. In the case of the father with the school phobic boy, for instance, after explaining the difference between rational and irrational thoughts, I might present him with a list of 20 irrational beliefs that he had about his son, himself, or others, and then ask him to change them to rational ones. For example:

IRRATIONAL: "BOYS SHOULD NOT BE AFRAID."
RATIONAL: Everyone is afraid at some time or another. Fear is a normal emotion and serves an important purpose when we are confronted with danger.
IRRATIONAL: "PEOPLE WILL THINK I'M A BAD PARENT IF THEY KNOW MY SON HAS PSYCHOLOGICAL PROBLEMS."
RATIONAL: There is no way to control what other people will think. To think of parents as 'bad' or 'good' is an oversimplification. All parents do some things better than others, and the great majority are 'good enough' to raise happy, healthy children. Most people know that raising children is a difficult task, and that having problems at some time in the child's life is more the rule than the exception. People who think otherwise are acting on their own irrational beliefs.

Identifying irrational beliefs and the more realistic counter beliefs is usually not enough to change the old feelings of shame, guilt, and anger that accompany the original belief system. Ellis (1973) has suggested that there is a simple A-B-C relationship which links our thoughts, feelings, and behaviors. "A" stands for the activity or circumstance that causes a rational belief (B), and a rational consequence (C) such as a feeling or action. However, if at point "B" the person has an irrational belief (iB) then he will also have an irrational consequence (iC) including: feeling anxious, depressed, self-hating, developing psychosomatic ailments (headaches, asthma, etc.), or relying on defensive behaviors toward others (resentment, blaming, rejecting, and so on). To change an irrational pattern (A-iB-iC) to a rational one (A-B-C), a technique such as rational/emotive imagery (Maultsby and Ellis, 1974) might be used. In the example we have been using, the father would be asked to imagine the worst possible circumstance (A) that he could, closing his eyes and concentrating on all the details of the visual image. Perhaps the father might report that a neighbor whom he feels very competitive with comes over to his house and mentions that he has heard from the grapevine that his son is seriously psychologically disturbed and he wishes to express his condolences. In the same conversation, he lets it slip that his children are all star athletes and brilliant scholars.

Now, as the father imagines this scene, he will no doubt begin to get upset, angry, guilty, envious, resentful (iC). Rather than discourage these feelings, the therapist encourages them, instructing the father to feel them fully. After a few moments, when the father would describe his feelings as very strong, the therapist then instructs him to relax, breathe deeply, and experience a diminishing of these emotions until they are just a minor inconvenience or irritability (C). At the same time, the therapist instructs the father to remember the rational beliefs (B) that he has worked out and to repeat these to himself.

The purpose of this technique, which is one of many developed by Ellis and his colleagues, is to demonstrate to the father that his emotions are under his control and to have him practice pairing a rational response and rational consequence with a circumstance he has identified as being very troublesome. Since this hypothetical "worst case" circumstance will never take place, lesser moments of embarassment about having a child with a problem will assumably be taken more easily.

I typically use several of the other techniques described in this book (hypnotherapy, cognitive behavior modification, and family therapy techniques) in combination with Ellis's concepts. The goal is always to promote acceptance of the child's problems through self-acceptance of the imperfect, vulnerable, and rewarding conditions of parenthood.

4

Innovative Behavior Modification Programs for the Multi-Handicapped

TYPES OF PROBLEMS

Aggressiveness; Classroom Behavioral Problems; Habit Control; Head Banging; Independence Training; Pica; Running Away; Self-Abuse; Self-Stimulation; Toilet Training; Work Adjustment.

Indicators

Individualized behavior modification techniques are appropriate for all ages of children and appear in some form in nearly every short-term, multi-method treatment program. By definition these techniques are used with problems that are both observable and measurable and that occur with relative frequency. "Innovative" approaches, such as the ones described in this chapter, are particularly useful for multi-handicapped children and adolescents, whose problem behaviors are complicated by mental retardation, and/or other organic syndromes.

Contraindicators

Behavior modification programs are always contraindicated for problems that may have an organic base until a complete physical examination has taken place. The use of behavior modification techniques would be contraindicated as a *single* technique when other significant emotional disorders exist, such as depression, anxiety disorders, schizophrenia, etc. (although they are frequently used as an adjunctive treatment with these disorders). Because "innovative" approaches to behavior modification are frequently controversial, and used with clients in residential settings, extreme caution must be used to safeguard the rights and well-being of the child or adolescent. If there is any question that a technique is controversial or potentially aversive to the child, then the complete program should be reviewed by an outside examiner who is familiar with the particular type of problem of the child, as well as with the applicable laws and ethical standards.

THERAPEUTIC PRINCIPLES

Behavior modification is more than just a school of psychotherapy; it has become a set of widely accepted principles and techniques used by nearly every clinician who works with children, no matter what his/her particular theoretical orientation. Even the psychoanalytic or humanistic psychotherapist will frequently find himself or herself describing the principles of operant conditioning to a parent whose method of discipline is not effective, or using a desensitization approach to help a child with a phobia. Although they may be using a different language to describe what they are doing, the principles are familiar behavioral ones.

Because behavior modification techniques have become widely accepted, I will not use this chapter to review the basic techniques that have been thoroughly treated elsewhere (see, for example, Martin and Joseph's *Behavior Modification and What to Do About It* for an introductory text). I will concentrate on less familiar approaches which have been used over the last five years with severely and multi-handicapped clients.

In recommending these techniques, I assume that the reader has not only a working knowledge of basic behavioral principles and procedures, but some practical experience as well, and yet even these qualifications are not enough. In consulting for a variety of schools, institutions and clinics over the last ten years, I have found that even the most straightforward behavioral programs have a 50 percent chance of being misapplied. For this reason, before proceeding, I would like to present some important reminders about the use of behavioral techniques.

Keep Accurate Data

Behavior modification was developed around the principles of empirical scientific investigation, and removed from this foundation it becomes a house without a means of support. Behavioral programs need to be based on objective data from beginning to end, and the data should be able to pass at least minimal criteria for being reliable and valid. The most common errors in data collection include: no baseline data is taken before the program begins; the targeted behavior is not the one being measured; the behavior that is being measured is not operationally defined; the measurement of the behavior is so difficult or awkward that it is eventually given up; there is no post-program measure to see if the behavior is being maintained.

The Design of the Program
Should be Simple and Comprehensible

The person who designs the behavioral program is rarely the one who carries it out. Usually programs are written by psychologists, but carried out by parents, teachers, and a variety of paraprofessionals. Unfortunately, this situation provides an excess of opportunities for miscommunication which can undermine the entire program before it gets underway. To avoid this, the written program should be brief and concise, and the concept behind the program should be clearly explained. If the person who designs the program neglects to consider the strengths and weaknesses of the one who is to implement it, he may find himself with a very pretty flying machine that won't get off the ground.

The Person Who Designs the Program and the Person(s) Who Implement It Must Work Together

The prototype for the relationship between the person who writes the behavioral program and the one who carries it out is that of architect and builder. One cannot work without the other. In the best and most effective behavioral programs there is a spirit of cooperation and comraderie, founded in a mutual commitment to help the child. There is no place in a successful program for elitism or competition.

The Behavioral Program Must Be Flexible And Yet Consistent

Even the most thoroughly planned program is still largely an experiment. Situations change rapidly, and there is always something new for the therapist to consider. But being flexible with the program is not synonymous with being inconsistent. Alternative techniques will invariably come up in implementing a behavioral program, and they should certainly be considered, but changes should only be made when they are consistent with the basic principles of the therapeutic program, when they reflect a logical interpretation of the data, and when they are consonant with the subjective experience of the people who are responsible for implementing the program.

Problems with the Program Should be Anticipated

Sometimes behavioral programs don't work, at least not to the extent that we had anticipated. There are many reasons for this and finding them out may be the greatest value of the program. In designing the program, the therapist must consider all the variables that will help it succeed and all the ones that might impede it. He/she should use these to set the criteria for changes and for the eventual termination of the program. But if the criteria are not met in the specified amount of time, then the therapist should be ready with previously discussed alternatives. Planning alternatives, however, is very different than planning for failure. As we shall see in this chapter in the case of Ronnie M., it involves careful consideration of the potential for change of both the client and his or her environment.

These "reminders" hold true for all behavioral programs, but they are particularly important when working with the multi- and complexly handicapped child or adolescent. Although these clients represent a very small percentage of the number of children with psychological disorders, they have become a particular concern to psychologists over the last few years due to the nationwide trend toward deinstitutionalization and increasing fears about the adverse effects of the psychotropic medication. As a result, public and private institutions, parents, advocacy groups, and even the judicial system are looking to psychologists for help.

As more severely handicapped youngsters (and of course adults, too) are placed in community settings, they naturally have a wide variety of adjustment problems. Some learn to live in small group homes and commute to a school or sheltered employment in just a few weeks. But others have severe behavioral problems which, although tolerated and managed in an institutional environment, are unacceptable in a community setting. These problems include self-abuse, excessive self-stimulation, aggressiveness toward others, pica, bedwetting and soiling, and a wide variety of idiosyncratic habits and mannerisms that make these clients difficult to teach and to live with.

Particularly challenging to the therapist are the intricate psychological, social, and ethical issues that must be considered when working with the multi-handicapped client. Aside from having multiple behavioral problems, many are non-verbal and may perform below a three or even a two year level according to standardized intellectual tests. If their behavioral problems have been severe, they may have suffered from institutional neglect or outright abuse, and probably will have been exposed to a variety of medications designed to "calm them down," some of which may have done more harm than good.

In addition, as in the two cases I will discuss in this chapter, they are often referred to the therapist at a time of crisis. Their community placement, chance for education, and job training may be threatened, as in the case of Cathy S., or they may present an immediate danger to themselves or others, as in the case of Ronnie M. In every example, there will be compassionate adults who care deeply about the well-being of the client. But if they are the parents, they will be emotionally exhausted from a mixture of fear, guilt, anger, and frustration. And if they are the on-line workers, who care for and train the client, they will almost always be underpaid, overworked, and feel unappreciated.

This is the typical situation in which the therapist is called upon to "set things right," and to succeed, he or she must come up with an innovative approach.

To be innovative, however, the treatment program will have to be more than just new. It must also be fresh and creative. It must be built on sound behavioral principles, but at the same time be responsive to the human needs of the client who is to be served. The truly innovative program is not bound by traditional thinking, but rather derives its ingenuity and originality by careful observation of the client's individual personality and style.

Innovative therapists do not settle on the obvious, nor are they complacent in regard to the needs and rights of the child beyond the immediate problem. They seek positive approaches to militate a change in the child's behavior, preferring to reward new behaviors rather than punish old ones, building self-esteem, and stimulating compassion and caring in the child's life.

The following two cases were selected for their complex and serious natures, and to demonstrate the importance of an innovative spirit as well as technique.

TREATING AN ADOLESCENT
WITH MULTI-BEHAVIOR PROBLEMS
IN A CRISIS SITUATION

Mary S. was a moderately retarded adolescent who when I met her had lived the most recent ten years of her life in a state institution. At seventeen, she was part of a large group of children and adults who were placed in community settings under a court order.

Although the motives behind the court-ordered deinstitutionalization were humane and correct, its implementation was short-sighted. The primary problem was that the court assumed that the same agency that had done an inadequate job in educating and caring for these clients for so many years could take up the difficult task of finding community placements and handling the problems that were bound to occur. As a result, the deinstitutionalization process had become a disaster for many clients, and Mary S. was a case in point.

When I met Mary, she was temporarily living with her parents, having spent less than 4 months in her assigned group home where they felt that they could no longer put up with her problem behaviors. After she was expelled from her community placement, the state agency responsible for her education and care wanted her to return to their facility, in spite of the deinstitutionalization order, deciding that she was not yet ready for "normalization." Mary's parents, on the other hand, felt strongly that she should not be returned to a facility which had been continually accused of inadequate programming for its clients, and certainly there was no reason to think that they would prepare Mary any better for life outside the institution a second time around. The two major goals of Mary's treatment were: to make her time at home productive for Mary and tolerable to her parents; and to prepare her to move into a new group home as soon as one became available.

The most extraordinary thing that first struck me about Mary was the laundry list of complaints about her. In the initial interview in her living room, in which Mary was present, rocking and mumbling to herself, her mother listed her immediate problems as: echolalia; pacing; an inability to stay with a group of her peers (this was the primary cause of her dismissal from the group home); foraging for food; unrestrained eating habits (gobbling up foods almost to the point of choking, which in turn caused obesity); mild aggressiveness in the form of pushing and charging at people who were in her way; picking at her skin, particularly around the mouth and on the legs; verbal and non-verbal self-stimulation (i.e., yelling nonsense words, repeating phrases or single words in a sing-song voice, rocking back and forth and running circles); a variety of ritualistic habits, such as making and unmaking the bed, or turning all the food on the shelf so that the labels pointed one way; getting up early in the morning and roaming around; and general obstinancy.

Mary's parents were gentle people in their late fifties. Although they had visited Mary every weekend while she was in the institution, they did not feel prepared to keep her at home except for a limited amount of time, and yet they could not bear the thought of her going back to the state institution.

The question was more where to start than what to do, so I sat down with Mary's mother and we came up with a prioritized list of her problems. Her constant picking at her skin came up as number one.

Facial Picking

We began with a program to get Mary to stop picking at her skin because it was the most irritating behavior to Mary's parents, because it had health implications, and because it detracted so much from Mary's appearance. She picked at her face constantly, presumably out of boredom and habit, unless told to stop. She had large welts around her mouth, swollen lips, and frequently had infected sores.

In deciding which symptom to treat first in such a complicated case, I had to choose not only one that was significant, but also one that had a good chance for immediate success. This was not only to demonstrate that behavioral programs could work, in itself important, but also to give momentum to the complex job of improving the quality of life for Mary and her parents.

Considering all of Mary's behaviors, her skin picking seemed to be one of the easiest to change. The behavior itself was discrete, and its effects were clearly discernible. From the initial interview with Mary's mother, I knew that this particular behavior came and went, suggesting that it was not completely intractable (as compared, for example to her echolalia, which was always present and remained at about the same level). In addition I observed that Mary already had developed some control over her picking. During our first interview Mary raised her hand to her mouth several times, and her mother was able to prevent her from picking by an admonishment or even just a raised eyebrow. This told me that Mary could interrupt the behavioral chain of the habit, and that she was willing to do so, with only a minimal cue, to please her mother.

The Program.   The program we used was a modified form of habit control, as suggested by Azrin and Nunn in *Habit Control In a Day* (1977). The primary elements of the program were as follows:

When Mary picked at her face, her mother or father were to say "No, Mary" in a loud voice, and sit her down in a chair for five minutes' "time-out." During this time Mary was to put on plastic gloves of the type used for dishwashing. At the end of the five minutes Mary was verbally praised for her cooperativeness and for her patience, and was then given lotion to put on her hands and legs (which were also frequently scratched) and a medicated cream for her lips. Again Mary was praised for her good behavior, and for this appropriate way of taking care of her body while deriving tactile stimulation. Finally, Mary was told to repeat the words "no picking," which because of her perseverative echolalia, she did several times.

Principles.   The principles of this technique worked because they were simple and straightforward. Breaking the process down, there were four behavioral tenets being applied:

Contingency Management.   The behavior of skin picking was not reinforced as it had been in the past. Time-out was used as a neutral response to the behavior and putting on the gloves was a mildly aversive response.

Symptom Substitution.   Azrin and Nunn (1977) suggest that to break a habit you must substitute another habit that fulfills the same basic psychological and physiological needs, but in a socially appropriate way. Using hand cream, facial cream and lip balm is certainly more appropriate than picking at one's skin, yet involves essentially the same areas of the body and the same motions, and can be done frequently during the day without harm.

Positive Reinforcement.   Positive attention for new, appropriate behaviors can never be overdone. In this case, it focused Mary (and her parents) on her successful achievements and helped build her self-esteem.

Symptom Competition.   Telling Mary to repeat the words "no picking" was an experimental use of Mary's echolalia as a cognitive mediating technique (see next chapter). Echolalia and other common perseverative uses of language are common in moderate and severely handicapped individuals, and there are several theories about their origin and purpose. It has frequently been observed that echolalia can be a form of self-control and might have some adaptive purpose.

In Mary's case I speculated that the repetition of the phrase "no picking" might have some inhibitory effect on the action itself. This use of one "symptom" or habit to counteract or compete with a more serious one can be extremely effective when used judiciously. The second symptom must be carefully selected as one that later will not become more maladaptive than the first, and must be a behavior which can be tolerated, even valued, as part of who the client is.

Data Collection.   Measuring two variables in the primary behavioral program provides the therapist with the most information about the effectiveness of the program. One should show an increase in positive behaviors, and one should reflect a decrease in the maladaptive ones.

The positive outcome in this case was Mary's clearer complexion. I asked her father to record this change by taking a Polaroid picture of his daughter's face every morning for ten days, and counting the number of discernible marks. This method of data collection took less than a minute a day and truly measured the effects of the program. In addition, it was a satisfying way for Mr. S. to interact with his daughter and to provide her with feedback on her appearance.

At the same time I measured the decrease in the targeted behavior by asking Mary's mother to mark on a 3×5 card the date and time of the day that the behavioral program was administered. This measure corresponded to the number of times that Mary was observed picking her skin and gave me a clearer picture of the relationship of the program to the actual improvement in Mary's appearance. It was expected that these two measures would be highly correlated—the less frequently the habit control program was administered, the fewer marks Mary would have on her face. These measures could have been related in other ways as well. If, for instance, the number of marks on Mary's face stayed high, yet the number of times that picking was observed began to diminish, then we would assume that the picking was being done at night or in private, and that the present program was ineffective. If, on the other hand, Mary's face began to clear, but the number of times that she was seen picking stayed the same or even increased, then we might assume that while some aspect of the program was working, Mary was using this behavior largely to get attention.

The data supported the effectiveness and success of the program (see Figure 4.1). Within ten days, Mary's complexion had almost completely cleared, and her mother said that "the problem was solved."

I stated things a little differently: "A good technique has been found." I cautioned Mrs. S. that the majority of behavioral problems of the multi-handicapped come and go; only a few stay away. What is important is that we know how to treat them when they appear, and we can almost immediately diminish their quality and quantity.

Stubbornness

Mary liked to do things when, and only when, she was in the mood, and because of her size and slightly belligerent nature, few people were ready to argue with her. I wasn't sure just how her stubbornness had been dealt with in the state institution, but in putting together bits of information, I concluded that not too much had been expected of her, and if she were in an obstinate mood, then she was just left alone to brood, make perseverative noises, rock, pace, or go through one of her ritualistic behaviors.

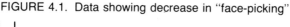
FIGURE 4.1. Data showing decrease in "face-picking"

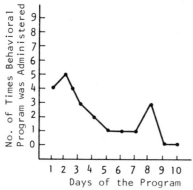
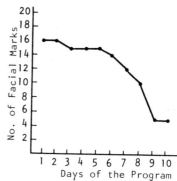

In her former group home these behaviors isolated Mary from the other clients and antagonized the staff. In spite of their patient efforts, they could not get Mary to leave her bedroom and had to leave a much needed staff member behind with her. It was this strain on their staff resources which finally made the situation intolerable. At home Mary was so willful that her parents were afraid to take her out of the house, for fear that she would run away (which she had done on several occasions), or cause an embarrassing scene.

On the surface, Mary's stubborn and recalcitrant behaviors may not have appeared too bad. She was petulant and threw childish tantrums, but she didn't really hurt herself or anyone else. But if we looked just below the surface we could see how her stubbornness had catapulted her into a crisis situation, where she couldn't move forward or backward. She was isolated and unstimulated—a prisoner in her own home. Decreasing her stubbornness became the focus of her treatment plan.

The Program.   To decrease Mary's stubbornness and increase her co-operativeness, I used a simple contingency management technique, rewarding positive behaviors on a fixed schedule and taking away rewards when she refused to cooperate.

To begin, Mary was given a small notebook with an attractive cover. Each page was to be used for a half-hour interval, in which time Mary could earn three Happy Faces for cooperative behaviors. However, if she showed any uncooperative behaviors at all, then she would have the smile of one Happy Face turned into a frown, or if no Happy Face had been earned, she would get a Sad Face drawn into her notebook. The program was to run from nine in the morning to nine at night and was administered solely by her mother. Mary's rewards for good behavior were in the form of dessert at lunch and dinner. If she had earned nine out of a possible twelve Happy Faces before then, she was able to get a dessert, which she looked forward to with great relish.

When Mary was given a Happy Face, her mother was to say, "Good girl. You've been very cooperative doing _____ (whatever the task was). I'm very proud of you." When Mary was given a Sad Face however, her mother was to raise her voice and say, "No, that _____ (the name of the behavior) is not good behavior. I will count to ten and if you do not stop by then, you will get a Sad Face, and if you get four Sad Faces, then you will not get dessert." If Mary did not stop her behavior by the count of ten, then her mother entered the Sad Face in the notebook, and took Mary by the arm and led her to a chair where she had to sit for three minutes of "time-out." If Mary were already sitting (usually on the stairs), she still had to get up and sit in a chair.

To administer this program only in Mary's home would probably have been the simplest strategy, but it would have confined the behavioral changes to an artificial situation. Mary didn't belong at home with her parents anymore; her appropriate placement was in a community-based group home with four or five of her peers. Mary's behavior could only be judged in community settings, so twice a week when I visited Mary in her home, we went on community outings—to the drugstore, to restaurants, to the grocery store, and so on. I encouraged Mary's parents to take her on similar daily outings as well.

As we had anticipated, Mary's behavior was less than ideal, but with each experience I learned more about how to anticipate her reactions. The first time we went out, within moments of our leaving the car, Mary dove for a trashcan and started rummaging through it. Her parents, confused and embarrassed, watched her until I took her by the hand and forcefully led her away. I immediately reminded her, "No! That is not good behavior. You must walk away right now or you will get a Sad Face," and I counted to ten. Since Mary would not walk away on her own, I entered a Sad Face in her book and reminded her that if she got three more Sad Faces, she would lose her dessert. What was significant about this experience was her parents' reaction, or, rather, their hesitation to react. There was a span of five or ten seconds between the time that Mary spotted the trashcan and moved toward it. This reaction time was critical. In subsequent outings, I learned that if Mary felt the strong presence of an adult, either physically or through a forceful verbal reminder of her Happy Face program, then she could control her impulses. However, if this time period passed, then to get her to change her behavior was likely to result in a confrontation.

It is this type of information about the behavioral quirks and idiosyncracies of the client that is most helpful in his/her habilitation—perhaps even more helpful than the program itself. My goal in working with Mary, as it is when working with most handicapped clients with multiple-behavioral problems, is to make even their most outrageous behaviors more acceptable by making them more predictable. As we can come to understand that every behavior of a client is an attempt to fulfill his/her basic human needs, then we can come closer to accepting them as complete people.

Mary's formal treatment program ended when she was enrolled in a group home for the moderately retarded about a half an hour's drive from her home. Although many of her behaviors would still have to be addressed, Mary was able to weather this important transition period, and, because of the therapy, was able to take a step forward in her life. In addition, the people who would now work with Mary were able to have more information about her than anyone had had before, giving her a much greater chance to succeed.

THE CHRONIC HEAD BANGING OF A 13-YEAR-OLD BOY

Ronnie J. was referred to me by a private special education school for his constant self-abuse. Diagnosed as severely retarded from birth, he began to bang his head and hit himself beginning at three years of age as a response to not getting what he wanted. Although many behavioral programs were tried in the next ten years, the severity and frequency of Ronnie's self-injurious behavior kept increasing.

His parents noted that Ronnie would go through periods lasting one to three months when his head-banging and hitting would be more intense. During this time they would keep his helmet on day and night and would put pads on his hands, knees, and shins. These periods seemed to coincide with any change in Ronnie's schedule: a new teacher in the classroom, a brother going off to college, moving him to another bedroom. As hard as they tried to keep Ronnie's life consistent and predictable, they never knew what might trigger these episodes.

Between periods of extreme self-abuse, Ronnie would be relatively quiet and easy to live with. Although he was severely handicapped, with developmental skills in the two- to three-year-old range and a vocabulary of only three words (yes, no, and his name), Ronnie was also friendly, affectionate, and very popular with the staff at his school. His educational program consisted of learning self-help and prevocational skills such as the ones he might need in a sheltered workshop. Even though his potential was limited, it was thought that at some time he could live in a group home where he could care for some of his needs.

At the time of the referral, Ronnie's self-abuse was so frequent that his school wasn't sure that they could keep him. Even when he was wearing all of his protective equipment, he was attempting to hit himself, wailing and thrashing out, nearly 50 times a day. They had assigned a teacher's assistant to spend all her time with Ronnie to try and reduce this behavior, but it was all she could do to keep him in the classroom. She couldn't control his self-abuse, and in spite of his padding Ronnie had bruises on his legs and arms and large welts on his face. If Ronnie's hands were free for a moment—to go to the toilet, to eat, to put on his clothes—he would strike. Since the beginning of this intense period of self-abuse virtually no training or education had been done, and the school staff was on the edge of despair.

At home, there were not many things that Ronnie enjoyed more than following his older brother or his parents around the house. He liked to watch them and to have them talk to him about what they were doing. In quiet periods Ronnie would reluctantly stay by himself and watch T.V. or flip through magazines. But at the times when he was agitated and self-abusive, he thrashed about in violent trantrums when left alone, knocking over tables and chairs, hitting his helmet against the wall, and trying to remove his protective padding.

In considering programs for clients who are self-abusive, I always assume the worst: someday they may irreparably damage or even kill themselves. For this reason I believe in leaving no stone unturned when considering ways to extinguish this behavior, and will often try approaches which I might find too controversial in other situations.

In cases like Ronnie's, where self-abuse has been going on for years, there is relatively little hope of eradicating this behavior competely. It is more realistic to see this as a cyclical problem, to train the people who live and work with the client to recognize the early signs of increasing self-abuse and agitation, and to be prepared with a full range of resources and alternatives that will immediately diminish the behaviors. To do this, I use the following questions as guidelines:

- What conditions in the environment will generally keep the internal and external stress of the client at the lowest level possible?
- In times of severe stress, what are the maximum resources that can be applied to reduce the self-abuse to an acceptable level, and protect the client?
- How can the client be trained and educated in spite of the severity and disruptiveness of this behavior? How can he or she be kept in a community placement?

Unlike the preceding case of Mary S., whose problems could be weighed against one another and treated one at a time, we did not have this luxury with Ronnie. There was only one important behavior to reduce, the number of times that he hurt himself.

In accordance with the multi-method approach, we used seven interventions simultaneously to produce the quickest effects possible. Rather than presenting these in their order of importance (for before we began we had really no idea which ones would be effective and which ones wouldn't), they are presented in the order in which they were implemented.

The Use of a Vibrator

A few studies suggest that self-abusive behavior can be reduced by replacing painful stimulation with pleasant tactile stimulation in the form of vibration. The studies hypothesized that these children and adolescents suffer from a lack of tactile and kinesthetic stimulation which they crave most acutely in times of boredom and distress (the same times that many of us also seek additional stimulation in the forms of eating, smoking, drinking, etc.). Although we don't know just why these clients choose such a primitive form of stimulation, it is assumed that they cannot conceive of how to get the intense level of excitation that they need by any other means than striking their heads and limbs.

But what if another form of stimulation could be provided, one that could be equally intense and point specific? If this type of stimulation reduced the client's level of physiological distress, rather than raised it, then wouldn't the need for self-abusive behavior also be reduced? In Ronnie's case, we attempted to see if an intermittent reinforcement with a hand-held adjustable, vibrating wand would reduce his self-abuse.

The vibrator was first presented to him in his school room, as he sat in his chair, clearly agitated, trying to hit one knee against the other in spite of his teacher's protests. I took the vibrator, turned to full strength, and with a mirror placed in front of him so that he could see what I was doing, slowly stroked his upper back and shoulders.

His response was almost immediate. He leaned back in his chair, and let his shoulders and back drop to a relaxed position. His whole body began to lose its tension. For fifteen minutes he sat there, nearly motionless, while I moved the vibrator over his arms and legs, watching for spots that might be more pleasurable or more irritating. Like most people, Ronnie seemed to enjoy being massaged most on his shoulders. He disliked having the vibrator on his arms and legs, possibly because it irritated his many bruises.

We decided to give Ronnie three five-minute periods of stimulation with the vibrator, at random intervals, every half an hour.

A Time-Out Room

Although federal and state laws have discouraged and sharply restricted the use of time-out or isolation rooms as a form of behavioral treatment, they are still used in many parts of the country, primarily with aggressive patients. Ronnie's records had revealed that a time-out room had been used with him several times in the past, with very dramatic results, as a consequence of his self-abusive behavior. At a group conference attended by his parents and the school staff, we decided to give it a try.

Replicating the treatment strategy that had worked in the past, Ronnie was to be led to the time-out room every time he hit himself, no matter how hard; he was to remain in isolation for two minutes. If Ronnie hit himself during his two minute period, he was led out of the room, admonished, led back in, and had to remain in isolation for another two minutes.

When I first heard of this program, I didn't think it made a lot of sense. I knew that Ronnie loved to be with people, but I didn't see how two minutes' removal from them would be a very significant aversive consequence. I also didn't understand why Ronnie wouldn't use the time in isolation to try to hit himself, and even though the rooms were well padded with no hard or sharp surfaces, I saw this whole procedure as a potential revolving door with Ronnie and the counselor going in and out of his small room all day. I expressed my misgivings, but bowed to the decision of the principal of the school who had known Ronnie when the time-out room had been used in another school. She said it worked, and so I went along with her judgment.

Within three days, the combination of using the vibrator and the time-out room had reduced Ronnie's self-abuse from nearly fifty times a day to two times a day. A second time-out room was built the following week in Ronnie's home and the same procedures were implemented.

A Change in Medication

During the ten years that Ronnie had been self-abusive, at least five medications had been tried in attempts to reduce this behavior. When I began the case, Ronnie was on a high dose of a major tranquilizer, which he was given regularly even though it was not having the desired effect and may have been making Ronnie more irritable. When I called up the neurologist that Ronnie was seeing, he frankly admitted to being confused about the whole case. The next day I advised Ronnie's mother to seek another medical opinion.

The second physician, a pediatrician who specialized in working with the handicapped, decided to slowly take Ronnie off the medication he had been using. Before prescribing anything else, he wanted Ronnie to have a "drug holiday," completely free of medication, to see what his baseline behavior was like.

A Change in Protective Equipment

In an initial conference with Ronnie's family and the staff at his school, the question of his protective equipment came up. There was a controversy over when Ronnie should wear it, what it should consist of, and by what criterion it should be removed. The school personnel felt that Ronnie should wear his equipment as little as possible, because they felt that it inhibited his range of motion and kept him from working at some tasks that he otherwise might be able to do. His parents, on the other hand, felt that the equipment itself helped quiet Ronnie down, and that with it on he felt "safe from himself." They mentioned that on several nights he had gone to bed very agitated without his protective equipment on, but that putting it on had an immediate calming effect and he was able to sleep through the night.

We finally compromised by having a member of the school staff find out about obtaining lighter and less bulky equipment from an occupational therapy specialist. However, since we knew that the old equipment did seem to calm Ronnie down, and since his bumps and bruises suggested that he still needed it, we decided to have him continue wearing it on a full-time basis.

Relaxation Training

One of Ronnie's teachers had read about the effects of relaxation training on the severely handicapped and had tried this several times with Ronnie. At the beginning of the day, when Ronnie arrived, she had him sit very quietly with his feet up and eyes shut, while he listened to soft music. After about 15 minutes, she approached him gently and guided him toward his first work task. I agreed with the teacher that this technique might have an effect in reducing Ronnie's agitation, and it certainly couldn't hurt. We decided on a program where Ronnie would relax for 15 minute periods, three times a day: in the morning, just before lunch, and in the early evening. I cautioned, however, that relaxation training should not be contingent on Ronnie's abusive behavior—that is, they should not try to calm him down by relaxation techniques when he was abusive. To do this would be to reward a negative behavior with a pleasurable response, and would certainly contribute to the maintenance if not an increase in Ronnie's self-abuse.

Positive Reinforcement and Choosing Appropriate Tasks

When I first met Ronnie, the staff at his school was using a single positive reinforcement program to try and decrease Ronnie's self-abuse. The program consisted of giving Ronnie raisins at 3 minute intervals if he did not hit himself. If he did hit himself, he was admonished, and did not get raisins.

Unfortunately, there were several flaws in this program. Although we knew that Ronnie liked raisins, we had no indication that this reward was strong enough to extinguish such a long standing habit as his self-abuse. In fact, data from this program showed that it had very little effect, and certainly not enough to justify the time of one staff member to give Ronnie raisins every five minutes. In addition, it was not clear whether admonishing Ronnie, and so giving him attention for hitting himself, was reinforcing his self-abuse or not.

My suggestion was to make positive reinforcement contingent on completion of a task, rather than on "abuse-free" time periods. It was necessary, in any case, for Ronnie to learn self-help and work skills. His teacher agreed to set up a hierarchy of tasks, from simple ones which Ronnie could do easily to slightly more difficult ones requiring more time and concentration. Ronnie got a reward whenever he finished a task in the alloted time period, whether or not he hit himself during that period. In this way we set up a second dependent variable to measure Ronnie's progress, rather than pinning all our hopes on changing one behavior. I emphasized that although the tasks should gradually increase in complexity, they should be designed to ensure success in getting a reward at least 80 percent of the time.

As I mentioned, by the third day of our program Ronnie had reduced his self-abusive behavior by 96 percent just by using the vibrator and the time-out techniques. So why did we keep on experimenting with other techniques? Because we needed to find a formula that would maintain this low level of his abuse with minimally intrusive techniques over the longest time period possible. Clearly we did not want to use time-out rooms indefinitely if some other technique would work just as well. Nor did we want to remove Ronnie's protective equipment if there was even a remote chance that he could hurt himself seriously. By combining all techniques at once, we wished to diminish the behavior to its lowest level possible, for at least a month. Then we would try eliminating the most intrusive and time-consuming techniques to see if Ronnie's abusive behavior began to increase again.

I should note that a strict behaviorist would probably do things the opposite way: considering one variable at a time, rather than confounding the results with a potpourri of techniques. This might be appropriate in some cases, but not when a child is in danger. Although we did not use the most scientific methodology with Ronnie, I believe we did use the most compassionate. Innovative behavioral programs begin and end with people caring about the person. When we add our imagination and creativity to this simple formula, I believe that there are very few children who cannot be helped.

5

Cognitive Behavior
Modification

TYPES OF PROBLEMS

Cognitive Mediation Technique: Anxiety Reactions; Aggressiveness; Habit Control; Hyperactivity; Impulse Control. *Cognitive Restructuring Technique:* Adolescent Depression; Underachievement (procrastination and study habits); Eating Disorders.

Indicators:

Cognitive Mediation: This technique was designed for children under the age of 13, who have not developed the use of internal thought to control their behaviors and older adolescents whose elevated emotional states (such as anxiety, anger, or fear) overwhelm their cognitive processes so that they feel out of control. Some children and adolescents who have intellectual or learning handicaps may also be able to use this technique to control their impulsive behaviors.

Cognitive Restructuring: This technique is primarily appropriate for adolescents who have reached Piaget's stage of formal thinking. It assumes that clients have developed the ability to have an internal dialogue, but that the things they say to themselves are based on faulty logic and produce mood states and consequent behaviors that are self-defeating.

Contraindications:

Cognitive Mediation: A significant deficit in the memory system would make learning this technique much more difficult and might undermine its effects.

Cognitive Restructuring: Since this technique relies on considerable written self-analysis, it would not be appropriate for adolescents who have difficulty in expressing themselves in written form, and/or to those whom the various "assignments" used in this technique would seem just another form of "homework."

THERAPEUTIC PRINCIPLES

In looking back on the history of psychotherapy in this century, we can first see a preoccupation with the emotional lives of clients, then a shift to where behavior was the sine qua non of the newer therapies, and now there seems to be a shift of interest to the role that the patient's thoughts and images have in the development and maintenance of their psycho-pathology. This chapter will address two of the major cognitive techniques that appear to have promise in the treatment of specific childhood disorders: the cognitive mediation technique, which assumes that certain types of children do not use their thoughts to control their actions the way that other children of the same age do; and the cognitive restructuring technique, which assumes that clients have age-appropriate cognitive structures, but that for a variety of reasons their thoughts are illogical or self-defeating and lead them away from purposeful behaviors that could bring self-satisfaction.

To understand the difference between these two techniques we might look at the role of cognitions, or self-statements, in learning a new physical skill, such as tennis. A novice player begins by taking a ball and a racquet out to the court, finding a willing partner, and swinging away. The main objective, she knows, is to hit the ball with the racquet and this she does in a fairly haphazard, but enjoyable way. But after awhile she begins to notice that her game doesn't look like the more advanced players she sees on the courts. She doesn't hit the ball as hard, or as low, or nearly as often. She looks and feels clumsy, so she decides to take a few lessons. What she learns from her teacher are *cognitive mediation techniques*: thoughts that she says to herself to help modify her behavior—thoughts to mediate her actions. After a few lessons, she goes out to the court, and now before swinging, she says to herself, "Keep your eye on the ball. Keep your knees slightly bent. Position yourself before the ball bounces. Step into the ball with your left foot for a forehand, right foot for a backhand. Follow through with your racquet." Our player practices and practices until these new movements become more automatic. When her game is poor, she knows that her form is probably off, and so she begins to talk to herself again, "Keep your eyes on the ball. Keep your knees slightly bent . . ."

Now our tennis player is really getting good, and she decides to start entering local tournaments. In many cases she is a much more polished player than her opponent, but she always loses. This is because of another set of statements that our player says to herself, which do not have anything to do with her learning of the game, but are the result of things she learned to think about herself when she was very young. Before a match, she automatically says to herself, "I know I'm going to lose again. I'm just not a winner. I want to win, but I'm so anxious that I choke." She begins to play, but even when she is playing well, she is thinking: "This can't last long. I'm beginning to get nervous. This is where my game begins to fall apart every time." And sure enough she becomes more tense and her anxiety level really does rise and she begins to swat the ball right into the net.

Our player has fallen victim to her self-defeating thoughts which have very little to do with reality of the game and certainly don't help her play any better. She says to herself before the game, "I know I am going to lose again," but how can she know that? She has never seen her opponent play and has no idea whatsoever of how either of them will exhibit their particular skills that day. This is an example of faulty thinking—specifically an overgeneralization, where previous negative events have become a "rule" of self-defeat. Our player begins her match on a note of self-pity and depression. She becomes doubting, insecure, and anxious, rather than enjoying the game and the benefits of the competition that she has chosen to enter.

The *cognitive restructuring technique* would have her learn to change her irrational self-statements into rational ones. A rational replacement for "I know I'm going to lose again" would be: "Well, I lost last week's tournament because I choked. But I don't have to do that again. I know I will play best if I just relax and concentrate. And if I don't win, it's no big deal. I'm really out here to get exercise and have fun."

USING THE COGNITIVE MEDIATION TECHNIQUE WITH HYPERACTIVITY

The cognitive mediation technique, first introduced by Donald Meichenbaum and his colleagues, has been most widely applied to overactive children who have a difficult time in school. In numerous studies, children who were labeled hyperactive were shown to be characteristically impulsive in the way that they solved problems. In solving mazes, for instance, hyperactive children would charge ahead as soon as they were given a pencil, entering blind alleys, cutting corners, and adding extraneous marks to the paper. Other children, who were not reported to have problems in the classroom, approached the mazes with a more reflective style, examining the alternative routes before they chose which way to go.

On closer examination, it appeared that the major difference between the trial and error style of the impulsive children and the analytic style of their reflective counterparts was that the impulsive children were not thinking about what they were doing—they just acted and tried to finish as quickly as possible. Basing his model on the work of the Russian psychologists Vygotsky and Luria, Meichenbaum (1977) hypothesized that hyperactive children, with their uncontrolled and frequently aggressive behaviors, had not developed an ability to use internalized speech the way that most children do by the time that they are five. While reflective children used an internal dialogue to solve a new problem or understand a new situation, impulsive children, like the proverbial frog, leaped before they looked. In further studies it was found that children identified as having behavioral problems in class were universally less sophisticated than their peers in decision making skills, in seeing alternatives, in generating hypotheses, in word attack skills in reading, and computational skills in math.

In developing a therapy for these children, Meichenbaum surmised that since these children were not less intelligent than their peers (all the studies compared groups that were matched on I.Q.), they must have a developmental delay in the specific use of their internalized speech to mediate and regulate their behavior. He patterned his technique on the way that children normally develop internalized speech, designing a four stage process to teach children to think about problems before they acted. Using a wide variety of visual and verbal puzzles and games, the therapist would demonstrate the problem first, saying his/her thoughts out loud. The child would then try the same problem, but rather than resorting to his usual trial and error tactics, he was to imitate the therapist's words exactly, and do just what he/she had done. In putting together a puzzle, for instance, a child might begin by saying, "Now I have to examine the pieces before I put them together. I'll lay them out in a row and look for two pieces that have the same color in them. If I see something on a piece of the puzzle that looks familiar, I'll make sure that the piece is right side up . . . ."

After imitating the therapist's thoughts at each stage of the problem, the child would then go through it again, rehearsing the same thoughts out loud as he worked. Then he would do the same, or a similar puzzle again, but this time the child would whisper the analytic, self-guiding statements to himself. Finally, he would do the puzzle one last time, but this time saying the words, which are now internal thoughts, to himself.

Although this treatment is based on a developmental pattern, its principles are more rooted in behavioral theory. The child learns to use self-directing thoughts just as if they were a new behavior. He models the use of the thoughts from a therapist whom he values and who reinforces him each time he uses this new way of solving problems. Like any behavior it is rehearsed over and over again, matched to specific environmental cues or antecedents, and slowly transferred as a new behavior to the place where the problem originally existed, the classroom.

Although the majority of research on cognitive mediation techniques has been done with hyperactive children, there have also been studies done with other populations who do not appear to use logical thinking to guide their behavior (see Meichenbaum, 1977). In particular, this technique seems to hold promise for thought disorders associated with schizophrenia, children with "state specific" anxiety (such as test anxiety), aggressive children, and children with impulse control disorders. The following examples show how this technique can be integrated into widely varying treatment plans.

IMPULSE CONTROL: A MILDLY RETARDED ADOLESCENT LEARNS TO CONTROL HER SEXUAL IMPULSES

Like other teenagers, many intellectually handicapped adolescents experiment with alcohol, drugs, and sex, but their lack of judgment and caution, in the form of internalized self-guiding speech, make them particularly vulnerable to the social and psychological problems associated with their adventures.

Alice B., for example, was a 17 year old with a full scale I.Q. of 73 and a level of academic achievement at about the fourth grade. Although her parents had several complaints about Alice's impulsive behavior, including her excessive drinking, her use of obscenity, and her truancy from school, Alice felt that these were not problems at all. She agreed with her parents, however, that she had a problem regarding sex. She couldn't say "no" to any boy who wanted to have intercourse with her, even though she felt that she was often taken advantage of by the boys in her school and her neighborhood. She had contracted venereal diseases several times, and was often teased unmercifully at school.

Alice's parents accepted the fact that she would continue to have sexual relations, but they wanted her to adopt some standards for whom she had sex with and where it would take place; naturally they didn't want to see Alice hurt. I was particularly concerned about the inherent dangers in Alice's lack of judgment and her inability to control her impulses. She would get into a car with nearly any man who pulled up and asked her to get in. She would have sex in abandoned buildings in dangerous parts of town, without any concern for her own safety. At least once she had become involved with a man who threatened her with violence.

For such a serious problem, I initiated a variety of crisis-oriented interventions, including family therapy and weekly consultations with Alice's school where she was getting group therapy and counseling, but for now, I will confine my discussion to the cognitive mediation techniques which were used to help Alice improve her judgment.

The first task was to find out just what went through Alice's mind when she was approached by a man. I devised ten pictures from magazine photographs and presented them to Alice to tell a story about each one, following the format of Murray's Thematic Apperception Test. Each picture showed a young man and woman in various stages of romantic encounters. Some pictures were clearly suggestive, but others were fairly neutral (e.g., a man and a woman sitting next to each other on the bus, but looking in opposite directions). I asked Alice to tell me just what each person was thinking, and I tape recorded her responses. The following response, which was given to a card which showed a close-up of a man and woman looking at each other, is a typical example:

> "The man and the woman are about to get it together. (*Therapist:* Do you mean have sex?) That's right. He's thinking, 'I wonder where I can lay this chick? In the stairwell? No, somebody will find us there. In the classroom? Yeah, we can find an empty classroom and do it on a desk.' And that's just what they did! (*Therapist:* What was the woman thinking?) Oh, she wasn't thinking about much. She kind of liked his wavy brown hair and his eyes, and thought he was a pretty good looking stud."
>
> (*Therapist:* What happened?) "Well, they went into an empty classroom and did it, just like the guy said. (*Therapist:* And then what did they each think and feel?) Well, the guy felt good and proud of himself, and said to himself, 'that is some good lookin' chick.' But the girl didn't feel so good about herself. She thought, 'Maybe I'll get the clap again. This guy probably doesn't even like me very much. I'll bet I'll never even see him again, and he'll go around bad mouthin' me and such.' "

On card after card Alice showed that she was totally preoccupied with the seductive words and behaviors of men and seemed almost unaware that she could have anything to say about whether or not the encounter was going to turn into a sexual experience. While there was no doubt that Alice was flirtatious with men in general, and probably more so when they showed some interest in her, she did not see that her coquettishness had anything to do with her problem.

The purpose of using a cognitive mediating technique with Alice was to get her to identify situations that might be potentially dangerous to her, and then to learn to say "no" and walk away as a matter of choice. We began by making a list of situations where Alice had had sexual experiences that she later regretted. These included:

1. A boy came up to me in the hallway and wanted me to have sex with him on the stairs.
2. A neighborhood boy wanted me to have sex in his garage.
3. A man pulled his car over, and told me to get in, and he took me to a parking lot and we had sex in the car.

We then made a list of the appropriate self-statements that Alice should have in each situation. For example, if a car pulled up to her and a man began to firt, she was to say to herself: "Any stranger who tries to pick me up in a car is up to no good. I won't talk to him, I'll just keep walking and look straight ahead. If he keeps on talking, I'll turn around and walk somewhere the car can't go and there are other people." In it's shortened form it became: "Look ahead—walk away."

Because I wanted Alice to practice these self-statements until they became automatic responses, I asked Alice's female counselor at school to come to her therapy sessions and act as a "model." First, I role-played each situation with the counselor, who said the new self-statements out loud. Then I role-played the same scenarios with Alice three times: first, she repeated the self-statements out loud; then she whispered them; and then she kept silent, but thought them to herself. We videotaped each situation and also looked for the non-verbal cues that Alice might be giving off that might encourage someone to continue pursuing her. If any of the tapes were not perfect, we would do the role-playing again.

Over a period of several weeks, we watched these tapes ten times. The object of this repetition was to strengthen the self-statements as conditioned responses, but it also helped heighten Alice's awareness of the problem and her responsibility to find a solution that was different than her former pattern of passivity, blaming her problems on everyone else, and suppressing all her thoughts and feelings about painful incidents. (For a comprehensive treatment of using cognitive/behavioral strategies to learn assertive behavior, see *Responsible Assertive Behavior* by Lange and Jakubowski, 1976.)

REDUCING ANXIETY AND AGGRESSIVENESS WITH THE COGNITIVE MEDIATING TECHNIQUE

Arthur was an example of a bright child who consistently performed poorly on tests because of his unorganized and erratic approach. He had a hard time following directions, frequently guessed at answers, and did not try to solve problems for which he did not have an immediate answer. The anxiety he experienced in taking a test made matters worse, inhibiting the analytic skills he showed in less pressured situations. Since spelling was Arthur's worst subject and since it was also the one where he was most frequently tested, this is where we began the therapy.

An analysis of Arthur's prior tests showed that out of twenty-five words, he only attempted an average of eighteen, but of those eighteen, sixteen (88 percent) were correct. To begin, I gave Arthur a spelling quiz in my office that exactly simulated the classroom tests. An analysis of a videotape of his performance looked like this:

> Word 1: Arthur takes ten seconds to think about the word before he begins to write. He writes out the complete word slowly. He is still

forming the last letters of the first word when the second word is read.

Word 2: Arthur hesitates thirty seconds before beginning to write the word. He appears to be trying to remember just what the word was, since he was not paying full attention to the examiner when it was read. He writes very slowly, and appears to be anxious. Arthur is only half-way through the second word when the third word is read.

Word 3: He is still working on the second word. He writes the end of the second word out even slower, as if this denies the fact that another word has been presented. He does not attempt Word 3 at all. He appears lethargic and looks up at the examiner, sheepishly, in readiness for Word 4.

This general pattern repeated itself for the remainder of the twenty-five-word test, with Arthur leaving six words out, but correctly spelling 80 percent of the ones he attempted.

The therapy program for Arthur was aimed at trying to get him to write his words faster; to leave a word unfinished if the examiner was going on to a new one, and come back to the unfinished word later; and to stress the importance of attempting every word. The following self-statements were taught:

Before the test:

"Work quick. Write quick. Listen carefully."

On hearing a new word being presented:

"STOP! Listen to the new word. Write it quickly."

On having a few moments pause after an easier word:

"Quick. Go back to the last incomplete word. Say that word to yourself. Finish it quickly."

Once these statements were learned by imitating the therapist, Arthur was shown the original videotape and asked to identify the places where these new thoughts should occur. When he did so, the tape was rerun in slow motion, and he had to repeat the correct self-statement, first out loud, then whispering it, and then thinking it to himself. This process was then repeated for a new list of spelling words, delivered in groups of five. On the first set of words, the therapist identified where the self-statements should go and said them out loud. On the second set of words, Arthur said them out loud. On the third set he whispered them to himself. On the list of words he had written eighteen out of the twenty words presented to him; all were correct. The two he missed were started, but incomplete. His score was 90 percent.

While anxious children are typically overreactive to their internal cues, the reverse is true for aggressive children who are so attuned to their environment that their responses appear to be reflexive. Aggressive children are often in a constant state of readiness. One hint of any angry feeling or a word about fighting and their dander is up. For this reason, role-playing or other stimuli that might evoke an aggressive response should be avoided in favor of approaches that desensitize the child.

Eddie S. arrived at a rural school in Colorado after having been raised for nine years on the streets of Chicago. To establish himself in the pecking order of his fourth grade class and also to draw attention away from his problems in reading, Eddie fought at least once a day. After having been suspended from school three times in one month, he was referred for psychological help.

The goal of Eddie's treatment program was to help him establish an identity for himself that did not focus on such a limited view of what he was and could be. But my immediate concern was to get him to stop fighting. I explained to Eddie that his fighting would eventually cause serious harm to himself or someone else, that he was in danger of being expelled from school (which might mean that he would be sent away to a boarding school), and that he was even beginning to get a reputation with the local police. As a positive incentive to change, Eddie won a chip for every day that he didn't fight; he could cash in the chips with his father at the end of the week, and either save his money or take it to town to spend.

The therapy program was carried out at Eddie's school in thirty-minute sessions twice a week. In the small room that also doubled as the infirmary, I had Eddie recline in a cushioned chair, asking him first to relax the small muscles in his feet, then the muscles moving up his legs, the muscles in his fingers, forearms, upper arms, and shoulders, and finally the muscles in his chest, head, and face. This relaxation process took about seven to eight minutes. Then I asked Eddie to imagine himself in various scenes as if he were looking at a movie in his mind. The scenes were adaptations of his fights, luridly described to me by his teacher. At the point in the scene where Eddie would usually fight, however, I had him say, "I'm not going to fight. My muscles can relax. I can win this one by walking away." Eddie was then to visualize himself walking away from the fight and to see a crowd of proud faces (including his friends, his father, and myself) cheering him on his "victory." As in the other examples of the cognitive mediation technique, Eddie repeated the scene and the new self-guiding thoughts three times: first out loud, then in a whisper, and finally as a thought. We usually ended each session by reading short vignettes that I brought in about heros who showed their bravery by walking away. As part of Eddie's program, I had his parents strictly limit his T.V. watching, completely eliminating all violent shows.

THE COGNITIVE RESTRUCTURING TECHNIQUE: NEW HOPE FOR TREATING DEPRESSION

The cognitive restructuring technique, unlike the cognitive mediating techniques just described, assumes that clients are constantly thinking about themselves and what they do. These thoughts, which include perceptions, attitudes and beliefs, determine many of the moods that they have, and these moods motivate specific behaviors. The thoughts of depressed clients, however, are invariably based on faulty logic. Their thoughts, or self-statements, serve to keep them depressed and inhibit behaviors that might improve their sense of self-worth. Common thought distortions of depressed patients include: over-generalization, absolute thinking, focusing on negative details, disqualifying positive occurrences, minimizing or maximizing the importance of events, and over-personalizing the reactions of others.

Dr. Aaron Beck and his team at the Center of Cognitive Therapy at the University of Pennsylvania School of Medicine have developed a method of cognitive therapy which restructures the distorted automatic thoughts of depressed patients so that their moods and behaviors become more aligned with the realities of their experience.

The techniques developed by Dr. Beck et al have been developed primarily for the treatment of depression, sometimes referred to as the common cold of psychiatric disorders. Usually lasting only three months, Beck's procedures for treating depression consist primarily of a series of paper and pencil exercises which are first done with the therapist and are then practiced at home. A paradox of this technique is that although the depressed patient characteristically wants to withdraw and become inactive, the therapy must require diligent and constant work that is entirely the patient's responsibility to accomplish.

To change the thought distortions of his patients, Beck teaches them to identify automatic self-statements and to "talk back to them." One method for doing this is the "triple column technique," requiring the patient to write down his/her self-critical thoughts, to label the type of distortions that these thoughts indicate, and finally to give a rational response, or rebuttal, to these thoughts. For instance, the following chart was done by Stacy C., a depressed and withdrawn adolescent who felt that he was not wanted by his family and rejected by his peer group at high school:

AUTOMATIC THOUGHT	COGNITIVE DISTORTION	RATIONAL RESPONSE
1. I'm all alone in the world.	This is the way I feel, but it is not really true.	I feel lonely, but there are many people I care about, and who care about me. But I still feel I want more. There are things I can do about this.
2. I'm doing lousy in school. There is no reason to try and study harder and go to college.	I am maximizing my failures.	I'm doing poor in some subjects, but well in others. Everyone has strengths and weaknesses.

FIGURE 5.1. The Triple Column Technique

In the cognitive restructuring technique, it is the therapist's job to represent an undistorted view of the world and the way it works, but adolescents like Stacy may find this hard to accept. As part of their struggle to form their own separate identity, teenagers characteristically reject the viewpoint of adults. This will be an issue in every type of adolescent psychotherapy, but it is particularly critical in a directive psychotherapy such as Beck's, where the therapist appears to be telling the client "how to think."

But this is only an appearance. It is *not* the therapist's job to tell the adolescent what to think, but only to point out a rational way of thinking which is free of distortion. Rational thoughts are based on fact, not on opinion. They should reflect the way that things are, not the way that the therapist wants them to be. Rational statements are objective, and, at least in principle, they can be proven.

For instance, take Stacy's automatic thought, "I'm all alone in the world. Nobody cares." I interpreted this distortion as an example of "disqualifying positive events." In fact there were many people who cared about him and showed it in various ways. Even his family, who criticized him harshly, did many things to express their love and understanding. To prove this, I directed Stacy to fill in a sheet for three days of all the positive things that people did which showed that they cared. I explained that this could include anything from a friendly smile and a hello to the unsolicited gift of a solid gold Cadillac. I told Stacy that there was no need, yet, to change the way that he responded to other people if he didn't want to, but that he did need to be completely honest and diligent in recording every positive incident that occurred.

At the end of three days, Stacy brought in a list of 132 positive things that had happened to him. Just a few examples are:

"The doorman said hello. (5 times.)"
"Mom fixed my favorite supper, because she said I looked frail."
"Joan asked me to eat lunch with her and Peter and Sam."
"Mr. Thomas (English teacher) said he liked my composition, and that I was 'an original wit.' Ha ha."

This exercise, like the many others in the cognitive restructuring technique, was designed to replace automatic self put-downs with new, rational self-statements which are grounded in verifiable facts. In Stacy's case, every time he thought, "I am all alone in the world, Nobody cares," this would stimulate a mood of self-pity and depression that in turn would lead to more social isolation, lethargy, and passivity. But now the behavioral chain was different. When he felt alone and uncared for, he would think of the rational response he had learned in therapy and remember the exercise where he realized that this was an unrealistic attitude. Rather than generating a cycle of depression and withdrawal, he would instead ask himself, "What made me think that? What triggers these automatic thoughts?"

At this stage of therapy, the client may be directed toward a slightly more sophisticated form of self-analysis using the Daily Record of Dysfunctional Thought developed by Beck. This form is an analysis of the behavioral chain which links self-critical thoughts to depression and inertia. It directs clients to consider what might have triggered their self-critical thoughts, what specific emotions the thoughts are associated with, and to what extent rebutting the self-criticism with rational self-statements helps in reducing the emotions associated with the depression.

As an example of this expanded form, we might look at another set of Stacy's automatic self put-downs, as he recorded it on his Daily Record of Dysfunctional Thought.

While Beck's therapy is designed to alter the way the patient thinks about himself, there are also other behavioral techniques involved in this method, giving it added power. The Daily Record of Dysfunctional Thought Form serves to focus the patient on the antecedents as well as the consequences of the behavior (i.e., the automatic thoughts) that are to be changed. The emphasis is on what can be observed and what can be quantified (the rating of the patient's emotions).

Date & time	Situation that pre-cipitated the emotion	Emotions 1. Specify exact emotion 2. Rate degree of emotion 1-100%	Automatic thoughts	Cognitive distor-tions	Rational response	Outcome Specify & rate emotions 1-100%
Dec. 10 7 P.M.	Studying for phy-sics ex-am. Ma-terial is very hard. Can't concen-trate.	Discour-agement. Apathy. Depres-sion. <u>Blah.</u> 90%.	I'm stu-pid. I'll never amount to anything.	Magnifi-cation.	So I'm not so hot in physics. I'm get-ting an A+ in English & maybe in French. But if I don't back away at this crap, I'll flunk!!	Discour-agement 40%. Impatient 10%.

FIGURE 5.2. Excerpt from Stacy's Daily Record of Dysfunctional Thought

The underlying principle of Beck's rating scales is his hypothesis that depressed people need to act in order to start feeling better about themselves. Apathy and lethargy are common symptoms of depression which contribute heavily to the patient's cycle of self-defeat. While a traditional psychoanalytic approach would emphasize under-standing the unconscious conflicts causing the depression before en-tering any new endeavors, the cognitive restructuring technique rec-ommends action as a way of breaking the reciprocal negative relation-ship between a patient's thoughts, feelings, and behaviors. The apathy of depressed patients is seen as part of their cognitive distortions. They devalue their positive experiences, overgeneralize their negative ones, and require perfection of themselves and everyone around them. Their inactivity and social withdrawal feeds their cognitive distortions that they are worthless and deserve no better than what they have. To break this spiral of defeat, patients must force themselves to be active, by planning every hour of the day if necessary. Stacy couldn't imagine anything else that he could do beside sit in his room and watch T.V. or listen to his stereo. But I impressed on him the importance of keeping busy, even if it seemed to him that he was just marking time. Our dialogue went something like this:

STACY: Why should I do anything anyways? Nothing I ever do is fun and there is no one to do it with anyways.

THERAPIST: You're basing this attitude on more distorted thoughts, aren't you? Watch the word "nothing." How can "nothing" be fun? There are half a million people who are playing tennis right now. Thousands are playing chess. How many at movies, swimming, at the library, walking, sailing, practicing an instrument . . . ?

STACY: Please stop. I get your point.

THERAPIST: You are also using some faulty information you have about the nature of emotions. You seem to think, "because I feel it, it must be true." But as we have seen, your emotions, while they are certainly important, are not the same as facts.

STACY: (Smiling) Right again, Doc. But what would you do if you were me? You probably have a million girlfriends and a private plane waiting for you at the airport to take you to your yacht in the Bahamas. But what about me? I can't even drive.

THERAPIST: Your teasing me is revealing. You know that exaggeration makes for good humor. Your jokes tell me that you can tell the differences between distorted thinking and reality. Perhaps comedy is an interest of yours. I've noticed that you like to crack a lot of jokes, and I've seen you in the halls of the school with a crowd of people around you while you dropped one-liners.

STACY: Yeah, I like to crack a few. I'd like to write jokes for Johnny Carson someday.

THERAPIST: It sounds like we may be getting close to finding an activity that you would enjoy. Reading on the history of humor? Writing down gags? You might even be able to sell them. There are plenty of good movies around. How about the new Woody Allen . . .?

STACY: OK, Doc, you got me. Just please stop talking. I'll do something. I swear it!

By the time this playful session was over, we had filled an activity schedule for the upcoming weekend, with several new things for Stacy to try, and of course many mundane tasks as well. After a few weeks of this, Stacy settled into a more active schedule and rarely complained of being bored or feeling all alone. I pointed out that it is perfectly normal to feel this way some of the time.

Another one of the many behavioral principles that Beck et al (1979) have built into their therapy is data keeping, to keep track of the severity of the depression. The Beck Depression Inventory (BDI) is a twenty-one question rating scale that can be filled out in a matter of minutes, and yet research suggests that it gives an accurate reading of the client's level of depression. Used a minimum of once a week and as often as once a day, the BDI gives the therapist and, of course, the client a clear indication of whether the therapy works. In Stacy's case, his BDI score changed from a 23 at the beginning of treatment (in the range of moderate depression) to an 8 by the end of our time together (in the range of normal mood ups and downs).

Although the majority of research on cognitive restructuring techniques has been done with depressed patients, this technique also holds promise for other disorders characterized by extreme mood states and maladaptive behaviors. Similar treatment methodologies to the ones I have described have also been used with eating disorders and with several types of phobias, and an even wider application of these techniques may be on the horizon.

The Video Self-Modeling Technique

TYPES OF PROBLEMS

Adjustment Training for the Handicapped; Assertiveness Training; Communication Training; Self-Help Skills; Reading Disabilities; Habit-Control.

Indicators

Although this is a very new technique with a limited field testing, it seems to have potential for a wide range of children as young as two years old, and with no specific age limit. This technique is often implemented without the therapist present, making it very cost-effective for clients who need a lot of repetition in their learning. Since almost all children are fascinated with T.V. and video technology, this is a particularly stimulating technique for the poorly motivated child or adolescent.

Contraindicators

This technique would not be appropriate for children who dislike watching T.V., such as some hyperactive children, and some children with autistic or schizophrenic disorders. A more common contraindicator is when children don't like seeing their image on T.V. This is often a characteristic of extremely withdrawn children and adolescents who are self-conscious about their appearances.

THERAPEUTIC PRINCIPLES

It is 7:00 p.m. and time for therapy to begin. Alex S. is sitting in his living room, alone. The lights are dimmed. Relaxed and yet eager, he turns on the T.V. and therapy starts. Loud rock music fills the room and Alex starts tapping his foot. His shoulders begin swaying to the beat and his hands pick it up. The title of the show comes on, as the beat gets even faster and louder—IT'S THE ALEX S. VARIETY SHOW—STARRING ALEX S. AND A CAST OF SEVERAL . . . the letters wander and flash across the screen, then fade . . . WRITTEN AND PRODUCED BY ALEX S. . . . in large red letters set against a blue background (Alex's favorite colors). Now the music begins to fade . . . WITH THE VOICE OF DR. L. SHAPIRO. The music fades more and a scene comes on the screen. It's Alex in a bar with two other young men. The other two teenagers appear to be chain-smoking cigarettes. Alex is not. His friends have several empty beer bottles and dirty glasses lined up on their side of the table. Alex is munching loudly on a hot dog, drinking a coke . . .

The video self-modeling technique created by Michael Greelis and Betsy Haarmaan (see ABC's of Video-Therapy, 1980) is an imaginative blending of the latest video technology and basic principles of behavior modification. Although the video camera and monitor have become more and more commonplace in the treatment of a wide variety of psychological disorders, edit controllers, character generators, and tape recorded overdubs are new to the psychologists' armament of tools. And yet the video modeling technique is based on one of the classic studies in behavioral psychology by R. Bandura, who demonstrated that children left alone in a room will imitate the aggressive actions of other children that they see in a home-made movie.

Since the Bandura research, hundreds more studies have suggested that watching T.V. can have profoundly disturbing effects on the attitudes and behaviors of children and yet there has been relatively little attention paid to the potential positive therapeutic effects of this symbol of modern technology. Now that videotape recorders and cameras have become as affordable as home movies, we must consider that the same principles that have been selling sugar coated cereals can be used to help change habits, learn new social skills, teach reading, and even help an autistic child acquire language.

The basic format of the video self-modeling technique is to present the child or adolescent with a *corrected* image of himself/herself performing some new learning objective or therapeutic goal. Imagine a girl who cannot pay attention in a group watching herself on T.V. The image on the screen shows her sitting attentively in her classroom, making constant eye contact with the teacher or whoever is talking. She doesn't fiddle with her papers or rest her head on her desk. For the entire ten minutes of the video-film she sits with rapt attention, eager to listen and participate. But how can this be, when this same child was observed that morning with the same teacher in the same small group, looking as if her thoughts were on another planet? Enter the technology of videotape editing.

It is surprisingly simple to produce a videotape that can serve as a self-model for a child. First the client is taught some new way to behave or to cope with a problem and then he/she is videotaped. The original videotape is then reviewed by the therapist and the desired performance is edited onto a new tape; undesired behaviors are left out. When the editing process is completed the client will have a powerful image of what he/she will look like when the therapeutic goal is achieved.

Seeing your own image is in itself highly rewarding, but the effect becomes amplified when you see yourself doing and saying the kinds of things that meet the expectations of the important people around you. Imagine the pride of an aggressive 8-year-old who has never been able to walk away from a fight, and now suddenly sees himself able to do it. Or a child with a learning disability who has refused to read her compositions in front of the class, and now suddenly she is able to show the class a videotape of herself, edited and overdubbed to emphasize her confidence and the self-assurance of her posture.

Even more exciting is the opportunity to build in reinforcers into the edited tape itself, reinforcers that accompany each new "corrected" behavior. The reinforcers can range from simple praise from the therapist, recorded while the tape is being made, to subtle techniques that would make a Hollywood producer salivate. In the example that introduced this chapter, the "Alex S. Variety Show," the videotape was made by a seventeen-year-old learning disabled young man who wanted to be able to resist the temptations of his peer group to smoke, drink, and take drugs. The tapes showed a series of vignettes of Alex and other members of his therapy group acting out situations where he had been enticed into these unwanted habits, but previously he had been unable to say, "No." In individual and group therapy, Alex had opportunities to learn new techniques to increase his assertiveness and to get consistent support for finding his own identity and being accepted for himself (which included his handicap in learning).

Every aspect of the videotape production converged to help Alex not only change the complaint behaviors he disliked, but to give him the opportunity to express and value the characteristics that made him unique. Alex had a hand in each stage of the video production. He wrote the scripts, directed and rehearsed the other actors, selected the music and the titles, and even helped in the editing. He selected parts of the filmed tape which he thought demonstrated his self-reliance and his ability to stick to his views, and edited out aspects of his behavior—slips of the tongue, hesitations, non-verbal gestures—that he felt were indicative of his "pasty old self!"

The final product, which was surprisingly slick, consisted of five ten-minute films. One showed Alex walking down the street approaching a jive gang he had known, and to demonstrate his swagger and newfound cockiness, Alex edited in a clip from a Humphrey Bogart movie which showed Bogart walking down the street in a strikingly similar scene. In another film, the voice of a girl in Alex's therapy group was dubbed in repeating a comment that she had made in group: "You're gettin' your shit together, kid."

While the preceding example demonstrates some of the more sophisticated uses of the video self-modeling technique, the mechanical and technological knowledge required to produce these tapes is surprisingly small. The use of a videotape recorder (preferably a portable model) can be learned in less than an hour, and good quality tapes can be made almost immediately with the basic equipment. Audio dubbing consists simply of plugging in a microphone to the videotape recorder and talking or playing music while the tape is running on "record."

Editing is a little more complicated, but can still be mastered in two or three hours. Unlike film editing, there is no splicing and mending involved. Segments as short as a single image are recorded on a second page in whatever order the editor wishes, with the original or raw tape staying intact (see Figure 6.1).

The editing process involves three basic steps: 1. Select the material that you wish to use on the final tape by viewing the raw tape and marking down the position of each sequence on the tape, indicating the counter number and the first and last words of the dialogue of that sequence (see Figure 6.2). 2. Then record the designated sequences in a new order onto a second tape, using an edit controller. In this stage you are looking at two T.V. screens, the first showing what you have on your raw tape and the second showing the rearranged sequences that will be your final "show." 3. During the assemblage of the final tape, you can add a variety of special effects. For instance, titles can be added by filming homemade sign boards, that are then edited onto the final tape. If

FIGURE 6.1. Equipment for Videotape Editing

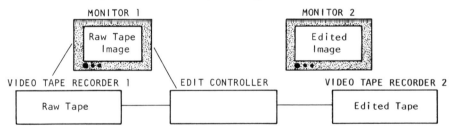

FIGURE 6.2. Log Sheet for the "Alex S. Variety Show"

Sequence No.	Counter Begin	No. End	Audio or Video Reference Begin	End
12	618	810	Alex walks in restaurant, says, "Hello, Guys"	Alex sits down at table; cut when he rests chin on hands
13	1003	1115	Pete says, "Whadda know, Buddy?"	Cut after close-up of Alex's smile
14	1301	1450	Alex says, "No thanks"	Alex sips his ginger ale. Add reinforcement here (dub in therapist's voice)

a character generator is available, it can give titles an even more professional look, allowing the editor to superimpose words onto any part of
the final tape in a variety of type styles and colors. New scenes and
images can be added by simply filming a few seconds worth of faces,
photographs, special objects, rooms, and so forth, and these shots are
then edited onto the finished tape. Clips from films or TV shows must
first be recorded off the air by the videotape recorder, and then they can
be added to the final tape like any other sequence. (It should be noted
however, that at the time of this writing the practice of recording copy-
righted T.V. shows off the air may be illegal in some or all states.)

Although the price for basic videotape equipment, including the
camera and the videotape recorder, is becoming more reasonable every
year, editing equipment can be quite expensive, and can double the price
of the initial investment. Most major cities, however, now have editing
studios where you can rent very sophisticated editing equipment by the
hour and edit yourself, or pay a slightly higher rate and have the people
who run the studio do it for you.

Repetition is the third principle behind the Video Self-Modeling
technique—repetition that usually does not include the presence of the
therapist. Depending on the nature and purpose of the therapeutic program, the therapy tape may be shown from five to ten times. After this,
even the best made tape gets a little boring. Tapes can be viewed on
consecutive days, once a week, or on whatever schedule fits with the
learning style of the client and the intent of the program. Many schools
now have videotape recorders as do many libraries and universities, or
as in Alex's case the tape can be viewed at home. If the family does not
own a videotape player, then one can be lent or rented to the family for a
short period of time. An advantage of home viewing is that parents,
brothers, sisters, and friends can also view the finished tape (assuming,
of course, that this is deemed to be appropriate by both the client and the
therapist), adding still another dimension of reinforcement for the child.

TECHNIQUES

An Aphasic Teenage Who Was Socially Isolated

The treatment of Ben S., a mildly retarded, aphasic adolescent, illus-
trates the multiple use of the video self-modeling technique. We used
this technique to help Ben with his communication, for socialization
and assertiveness training, to improve his hygiene, and even to help him
with his reading.

When 19-year-old Ben was first referred to me, he was a small,
wiry, unkempt young man whose speech was almost completely unin-

telligible. He was referred because his parents said that he had no friends, showed no interest in making any, and seemed to be more and more depressed. Everything about Ben seemed to be a study in contradiction. Although he was referred for withdrawal and mild depression, he was smiling and affable in the office. It was nearly impossible to understand what he said, but he talked all the time. His mother made sure that Ben always dressed in clean, well pressed clothes, but he wore them awkwardly, and he always appeared to be in need of a shave and a shampoo. Ben's intelligence was assessed to be in the mild range of mental retardation and he had demonstrated an above average interest and talent for electronics. He had even learned to drive a car and had passed the State licensing examination. But his academic achievements in reading, spelling, and math were only at the second grade level.

It was clear from the onset that this wasn't going to be a "talking" therapy, and yet I didn't see how Ben and I could accomplish very much without having some means of communication. After interviewing his mother and his former speech therapist, we decided that Ben should learn to use an alternative communication system to be combined with the communication skills that he already had. There are many types of alternative communication systems for aphasics, and each one has to be matched to the client's communication needs and learning style. Ben's new speech therapist wanted him to learn manual sign language because he already used many gestures in his speech, and since the American Sign Language method is a complete language, he would have an unlimited potential to express himself.

I, however, wanted Ben to learn to use a portable communication board. Communication boards consist of symbols, words, and letters which are mounted on some type of board. The client must only point to a symbol or sequence of symbols to get his meaning across. I argued that although sign language had unlimited potential for expression, because of Ben's intellectual deficits and poor performance in learning academic skills, we could not expect him to learn much more than a hundred or possibly two hundred signs and this might take years. In contrast, a communication board with iconic symbols combined with words could give Ben the same 200 word vocabulary with just a few hours of training. However, there were also good arguments against the communication board. It was awkward to carry around and use. It's uncommonness would draw attention to the handicap that Ben preferred to try and hide. (It later became clear that this was one of the main reasons for Ben's withdrawal. He would rather be alone than have people see him as abnormal.)

Finally, we decided on a compromise. We decided to try and teach Ben both alternative communication systems, to be combined with his intelligible spoken language and the fifty or so words that he could write. We reasoned that rather than choosing for Ben how we thought he would best communicate, we should give him the tools and let him make the choices.

Personal Adjustment Training

The Personal Adjustment Training Program (Zisfein and Rosen, 1971) was developed to teach developmentally disabled clients social skills that are important to their integration into the community, including how to get along with other people, how to make decisions and solve problems in a self-reliant way, and how to be assertive rather than acquiescent and compliant. These new behaviors are best learned in situations that are highly meaningful for the client, and for Ben this meant doing what made him feel most like the nonhandicapped people around him, driving a car.

In fact, a situation had occurred early in the therapy that under-scored Ben's need for better communication and social skills. He had been in a minor automobile accident in a parking lot, scraping a car as he left, but instead of stopping to talk to the other driver, he drove away. The police tracked him down later that day; fortunately, he was not charged with "leaving the scene of the accident" and was let go with a warning. Still, it was clear that this could easily happen again and that Ben would be in danger of losing his license.

With the aid of a co-therapist who did most of the training with Ben, we devised a scene in which Ben would have a "staged" accident on the street outside my office. Prior to the filming, Ms. B. worked with Ben on using his communication board, and taught him a half dozen easily understood gestures for communicating with the other driver. He was to explain that he had difficulty speaking, was sorry about the accident, and would provide his name, address, license number, and the insurance company's telephone number. Ben and Ms. B. role-played this scene until Ben could react with complete ease, even when Ms. B. (playing the other driver) varied her questions and responses. On the day of the shooting, I hadn't seen Ben for several weeks and I was surprised at how confident and excited he seemed. He inspected the camera and the portable videotape recorder down to the smallest button. He was de-lighted when I asked him to work the camera and film Ms. B. and myself in the office. When it was time to go outside, I asked Ben how he liked the idea of being a star of his own show, and he flashed me a huge smile, and the gesture for "A-OK."

The actual shooting took only about twenty minutes. We staged the tamest car accident in cinematic history, followed by a discussion between Ben and Ms. B., the two drivers. We didn't even need a retake. In fact, the scene was so good that relatively little editing was needed. After taking out a few of the extraneous words and motions, we had a perfect ten minute scene of Ben coping with a very difficult social situation. We had Ben select some background music from his record collection, juicing up the scene considerably. At an editing laboratory we reran several of the key points in the scene in slow motion, and I dubbed in comments that reinforced each of his new skills.

Since Ben lived close to my office, he came over to view his theatrical debut three times during the next week. On the third time, he brought a friend. This was the first social outing he had initiated in years.

Language Acquisition and Instruction In Reading

Since Ben had responded so well to the first video self modeling tape, we thought this same technique could enhance other areas of learning such as his acquisition of sign language. Ben was learning about 5 signs per week with his speech therapist, and we wondered if he couldn't double or even triple this rate. I arranged to tape a speech therapy session with Mr. J. and Ben, where he would be introduced to fifteen rather than the usual five new sign words. Rather than teach Ben the American Sign Language system designed for the deaf (we thought it would be too difficult for him to master) we instructed him in sign language culled from several tribes of American Indians. This system of gestures was reported to be 90% recognizable by the general public because of familiarity or because the gestures imitated the actions that they describe. To teach Ben sign language, Mr. J. would introduce the new words for the week, he and Ben would practice them for twenty minutes in his office, and then they would stroll around the vocational training center trying to use both the old and new words in context.

Reviewing the raw tape that evening, I thought of how a T.V. ad man might sell the same material. I thought about *Sesame Street* (at that time my daughter's favorite show) and the quick paced segments that repeat the same material in seemingly endless variety.

For the final tape I attempted to use the best of commercial T.V., rather than try to duplicate. That night there was a T.V. movie on that I was sure Ben would find interesting, aimed at a teenage audience. I called Ben and asked him not to watch it, for he would see it at my office in a few days. Then at the editing lab I combined the raw tape from Ben's therapy session with the T.V. movie, substituting scenes from Ben's language therapy as if they were commercials. At each point where a commercial had been, I introduced a new sign language word and reviewed the previous ones as well. By the fifteenth commercial all fifteen words were being reviewed; this continued for another ten "commercials." At the end of each new commercial, a fifty second blank space appeared, and my voice came on asking Ben to repeat the signs. He was then directed to check his memory by referring to a sheet (drawn up by Mr. J.) that showed pictures of hands as they formed each of the fifteen signs. Ben watched the movie in four segments, coming to my office after school. By the end of the week Ben was able to demonstrate all fifteen signs without error.

This method tripled the rate of Ben's learning, but the time-conscious reader who might have been counting the number of hours it took to make the tape might correctly wonder if it was really cost-effective. In this instance, I'd say that we broke even. In the traditional way of learning, Ben would have met with Mr. J. for three one hour sessions to learn the same material. For the tape, Mr. J. worked only one hour, but I worked two (one hour taping and another editing). For a second and a third tape which used a similar method, however, I wasn't needed at all, and the time that Mr. J. and Ben spent in their regular sessions was considerably more efficient. Because Mr. J. set up the video camera on a tripod, no cameraman was needed, and rather than spend the normal sixty minutes teaching and reviewing signs, Mr. J. was able to demonstrate and film new signs in ten minutes. Ben wasn't required to try and learn the signs at this time; this would happen when he viewed the tape. The other fifty minutes of "therapy" were spent editing the signs into a new T.V. movie that had been taped previously at Ben's request. Each commercial consisted of not only the ten new sign-words, but a review of the previous fifteen signs, edited in from the first raw tape (don't forget that unlike film, the raw videotape is never cut or used up and can be used over and over again). This second tape, taking just over an hour to produce, had the teaching equivalent of at least four hours (and of course we can't estimate how much more fun this way of learning was for Ben).

A third set of tapes was made with the help of Ben's brother James to improve Ben's sight-word vocabulary (words that are read entirely by recognition rather than by any system of word analysis). James, who was two years older than his brother, was invited to my office; and I gave both young men a short demonstration on how to use the portable video camera. Their assignment was to recreate a typical day for Ben, starting in the morning when he got up to wash and brush his teeth, and ending with the 11:00 P.M. news. In between there were the car ride to Ben's vocational training center, lunch at McDonald's, a drive around the neighborhood, an errand at the drugstore, and then the ride home again for dinner. For the tape they were to shoot five- to ten-minute segments for each scene. Ben was to film the background shots, and John was to film Ben doing the action. In each scene, I asked them to make sure and take close-ups of any printed words that it might be important for Ben to read. At home these might be labels on a vial of medicine or directions on the laundry detergent. On the road there would be street signs and directions to follow. At the restaurant there would be the menu to read, and at the drugstore there would be more signs to tell the customers where to find what they wanted, which items were on sale, and so on. I gave them written scenarios to remind them of what scenes to shoot and what kinds of things to look for (see Figure 6.3), and I reminded them that they only had two hours worth of tape that would be edited into a fifteen minute show.

We also spoke about how they would each feel about filming in public. Because Ben had spent so long trying not to draw attention to himself, I anticipated that he might find this public exposure too anxiety provoking. I was wrong. Both boys were enthusiastic about the project

FIGURE 6.3. Directions for Filming the "Drugstore Scene"

SCENE 1:   Ben entering the drugstore.
            Type of shot: Wide angle, zoom into Ben
            entering the door.

SCENE 2:   Shots of the signs above the aisles. Shoot
            each sign for about 20 seconds. Pan from one
            sign to the next if they are close. If they
            are far away, press the pause button until
            you aim the camera at the next sign. Shoot
            other signs as well: "Sale ... Do Not Enter
            ... Exit" and the like.

SCENE 3:   Ben going down the aisles, looking at the
            signs, examining various products. He keeps
            going until he finds the sign for toothpaste.
            Close-up of this sign. He picks up two
            tubes of toothpaste and examines them. The
            camera zooms in for a close-up of the price
            of each tube. Ben decides on the cheaper one,
            and he puts the other one back.

SCENE 4:   Ben pays for the toothpaste. The camera
            follows Ben to the cash register. Close-ups
            of any signs near the cash register.

and, like many exhibitionistic adolescents, were looking forward to being neighborhood celebrities.

A week later the tape was done, and I previewed it for ways to use it to teach reading. There were many good shots of new words to learn, nearly a hundred and fifty in all. I decided to edit the tape into four segments: at home, in a restaurant, in school, and on the road. Each section had a list of sight-words associated with it, complete with an introduction of each word, highlights of its use and context, exercises, and reviews.

Improving Personal Hygiene

I was reluctant to bring up Ben's personal appearance as an issue in therapy, assuming that he had more than enough reminders at home to tuck in his shirt and comb his hair. I had noted, in fact, that Ben's grooming had improved over the last several months, as he viewed himself more and more on videotape. While watching the tape that Ben and James had taken, a part of which showed Ben dressing in the morning, I realized that this segment might be a good opportunity to reinforce his new interest in grooming.

Everyone agreed that Ben looked great on the day he and his brother went out to film. That morning, while getting ready, Ben hammed it up in front of the camera. He shaved with the eloquence of a dancer, scrubbed his hair until every follicle glistened, and used his soap unmercifully. When he adjusted his tie in the mirror, he shone.

In editing this segment of the tape, I decided to emphasize Ben's grooming by slowing the action down and interjecting positive reinforcements that I thought Ben might find amusing and flattering. I taped one of Ben's favorite T.V. shows, about three beautiful female detectives, and chose several sequences which showed close-ups of them talking. I then asked three women to "lip sync" comments, that were flattering to Ben's appearance onto the tape. On the final version of the tape, there were just three ten-second segments of reinforcement for Ben's grooming, but these seemed to be enough. He was overjoyed with his new image and the humor of the tape, and watched this segment at least a dozen times. One day he brought two of his friends over to watch and they all had a good laugh. I couldn't help noticing that I had never seen Ben look so good.

7

The Developmental Game Technique

TYPES OF PROBLEMS

Hyperactivity and other Attention Deficit Disorders; Anti-social behaviors; Emotional problems associated with Developmental Delays, Learning Disabilities, and Mild and Moderate Mental Retardation.

Indicators

The developmental game technique was devised for children with specific developmental delays or cognitive deficits related to their emotional and behavioral problems, but it is also appropriate for non-handicapped children. Since it is a therapy which uses non-professionals as co-therapists to increase "therapy time," it is particularly effective when there is someone in the home, school, or institution who is interested in helping the child.

Contraindications

The developmental game technique would not be the treatment to choose when a quick intervention is needed, because it relies on a learning process which will vary with each child. It is generally not effective with children under the age of three, or with children who have not yet learned the rudiments of cooperative play, including an elementary sense of "rules."

THERAPEUTIC PRINCIPLES

The developmental game technique of child psychotherapy was created by myself and my colleagues at the National Children's Center, Inc., in Washington D.C., a school and residence for the multi-handicapped child. Clients referred to our programs had unusual combinations of emotional, behavioral, intellectual, and learning problems, and we were frustrated with the limitations of both conventional analytic play therapy and behavioral therapy.

Many of these children had received play therapy before coming to our facility, and the reports of these treatments were a litany of failures and discouragement:

> "Susan has not responded to three years of treatment. Because her language is limited, she is not able to verbalize the feelings and thoughts that seem to trouble her. Her play is stereotyped and characteristic of a much younger child . . . Her mental retardation appears to make her a poor candidate for continued treatment."

"Eric has not responded to treatment, and it doesn't appear that he will do so. Although he has made some progress in learning to play cooperatively with the therapist, this has not generalized to his home or his school, where he is still belligerent and non-compliant. Continued treatment does not seem to be indicated, and I would advise instead his institutionalization in a specialized boarding school that can deal with children who have similar problems."

Play therapy failed with these children because it didn't take into account the individual styles that handicapped children have in coping with the world. Many handicapped children have perceptual and language disorders, making it difficult for them to express themselves verbally or to learn from what is spoken to them. Many have cognitive delays or deficiencies, making them overly concrete and, therefore, poor candidates for dealing in the metaphor and symbolism that are the tools of traditional play therapy.

In 1975, when I came to the National Children's Center, the treatment programs for the children who had not been helped by play therapy were exclusively behavioral, but these programs were not enough. Like the play therapy that many of these children had experienced, the behavioral programs that were designed for them did not take into account their unique emotional and intellectual development. Most of these programs were administered in a group setting, denying these children the benefits of having just one special adult to care about them and respond to their needs. The behavioral techniques being used were helping to make these children more acceptable to society, but were not giving them the resources to make society more accessible to them. It seemed clear that an appropriate therapy for these children would have to look at their intrapsychic needs as well as their external problems, taking into account the unique ways that they developed.

There are several reasons why games were chosen as the most appropriate therapeutic medium for children with complex developmental problems:

• Learning for handicapped children is difficult and frustrating. Therapy should not be seen as another set of high obstacles. Games are used so that the therapy is perceived as "fun."

• Handicapped children are highly individualistic in the way they develop. The infinite possibilities of game construction allow the therapy to be molded to fit each individual child.

• Even mildly handicapped youngsters have difficulty in transferring what they learn from one situation to another. The therapeutic game can be played in a variety of situations outside the therapist's office and with other people who might be important to the child's development.

- In order to change, most handicapped children need more repetition than their nonhandicapped counterparts. Games allow a high degree of the redundancy that might not be tolerated in other kinds of interventions.

- Handicapped children are typically overwhelmed with the complexity of the world and their inability to make it respond to their needs. Games can be structured to guarantee success.

- A game can be a microcosm of a child's world and his or her problem. The game approach allows the therapist to create a manageable parallel to the child's concerns from where solutions can be magnified and extrapolated to the real world.

Choosing the Game

The strength of the developmental game technique lies in the thought and creativity of the design of the game. Each game is chosen to deal with one specific developmental issue that the child must confront, and should be carefully constructed using the parameters presented below.

Rules

The rules for the game might be very concrete and specific for one child, but more flexible, even changeable for another. The rules represent limits for the children, an important way for them to test reality. Most children try to break or bend the rules at some point, and the therapist's reaction is extremely important. The child with behavioral or discipline problems may hate to lose, and may try to prevent this by subtle or very obvious "cheating," but he must learn that while rules can be negotiated, once set there are consequences if they are broken.

The withdrawn non-assertive child, on the other hand, may be cowed by the rules. For these children the therapist may want to design a game where the rules are changed by the child as the game proceeds. Giving a child a voice in how the rules are determined forces him to act to make his experiences conform to his needs.

Frequently the therapist needs to revise the rules as the game proceeds with each revision bringing the game closer to its therapeutic purpose.

Attention Span

The attention span necessary to play each game must be carefully matched to the child in order to obtain the maximum therapeutic impact.

Even the best designed game will fall flat if it takes fifteen minutes to play and the child can only sit and concentrate for five minutes.

Most games consist of a beginning, a middle, and an end, with alternate "turns" between the therapist and the child until some specific goal has been achieved. This formula, however, is arbitrary, and a game can be played solely by the child in just a few minutes time if the child is not capable of more sophisticated social interaction. A dart game, a guessing game such as "Twenty Questions," or flipping a coin to get heads or tails, are just a few examples of games that can be played by the child who might not be ready to interact with the therapist. These games might seem too simple to be therapeutic; however it is rare for therapists to err in the direction of simplicity. More commonly therapists design overly complicated games that they want to play, but that do not mesh with the child's needs and abilities. When a game is too complicated or sophisticated for a child, the fact becomes evident in the first moments of play. There is nothing more frustrating than spending hours conceiving, designing, and constructing a therapeutic game, only to have the child become bored and wander off in the middle of it. To avoid this, the therapist should play a game of the child's choice as part of the evaluation process, noting the child's interest level, attention to the rules, frustration tolerance, and so forth. Actually playing the game is preferred to just asking a child what he or she likes to play, for children frequently exaggerate their own skills and ability levels and suggest games that they would like to be able to play, but that they have not yet mastered.

Still, there will be some times when even the most carefully designed games do not capture the child's imagination and interest. When this happens, the best avenue for the therapist is back to the drawing board.

Attractiveness

Most children prefer slick, commercially made toys and games, and may not be interested in a homemade game solely because of its physical appearance. For this reason, I advise therapists to follow the lead of toy manufacturers in designing games that are colorful and imaginative facsimiles of the types of games that the child might choose for himself. The initial interviews with the child should reveal the themes of the toys that the child is interested in (i.e., science fiction, super heroes, T.V. cartoons, and so forth), and this is usually a good place to start.

The unartistic therapist should not dismay. A trip around an art store will often produce ideas for graphic designs that require little or no artistic ability. Rub-on or plastic lettering can substitute for poor handwriting, magazine cut-outs can replace the need for hand-drawings, and new game boards can often be improvised from commercial ones with some construction paper. The therapist can also personalize a game the way a toy manufacturer never can, using pictures of the child, his friends, or family, or facts about the child's life.

Number And Types Of Players

One of the most important advantages of the developmental game technique is that while it emphasizes the role of the therapist in the careful design of the game, the technique allows other caring adults to participate in most games. (Some are best played by groups of children, usually with the therapist participating as well.) From the moment the game is first conceived, the therapist should ask himself or herself, "Who will be playing this game and under what conditions?"

Aside from "the therapist," the most common answer to this question will be "the parent," but sometimes it will be the teacher, a grandparent, or an older brother or sister. The other game players will be chosen according to their interest in and patience for the child's problems, their personality match with the child, their availability to the child, and their accessibility to the therapist.

Give even the most cooperative and psychologically sophisticated co-therapist some training. This is not out of a lack of trust for the co-therapist's abilities (and this needs to be made clear), but rather that the therapist has put in so much time and thought into the exact intent of the therapeutic game, it is nearly impossible to convey this intent to anyone else by words alone. For this reason, I like to videotape one or more game sessions that I have had with a child and then show it to my co-therapist with ample time for comment and criticism. If the therapeutic elements of the game are complicated, then I might also videotape the first game that the co-therapist and child play, again scheduling a meeting with the co-therapist for review and criticism. If there are still major problems at this time, these usually indicate that the game has been ill-conceived, and I would attempt to revise it or begin again.

Mobility and Durability

Since developmental games are frequently played in places other than the office, they should be compact and portable. Sometimes the child will keep the game with him or her, carrying it from home to therapy and back again. On some occasions a child may be playing the game at home, at school, and in the therapy room with as many as half a dozen different people, and so the game must not only be portable, but durable as well, and able to stand the normal wear and tear that children give toys. Since all toys are apt to get broken and pieces are constantly lost, I try to keep these facts in mind from the inception of the game. Whenever possible, the therapist should design games that can be quickly fixed or replaced.

Cooperation vs. Competitiveness

Most commercially made games are highly competitive and emphasize that there is always a "winner" and a "loser." More and more people, however, are writing about and designing cooperative games in which everyone wins and nobody loses (see, for example, *The Cooperative Sports and Games Book*, by Terry Orlick). Again, this is a variable that the therapist can control in order to focus on the therapeutic intent of each game. The therapist may want to have the game be competitive so that the child can learn how to lose. Or for an overly aggressive child, the therapist may want to design a group game where there can be no individual winners, and the only way that one child can get a prize is if all the children accompish some goal by working together.

If the therapist designs a game where he or she is in competition with a child, or where two or more children are playing and one clearly has more ability than the other, than the playing or the scoring of the game must be rigged so that each player has exactly the same chance of obtaining points as the other. This is usually best done by "handicapping" the player of greater ability (having a right-handed player play a target game with his or her left hand). However, adjustments should never be falsely made to give a child an extra advantage, even if his luck is bad and he keeps losing. The object of this type of change is to equalize the game, not to distort reality.

Rewards

By definition all therapeutic games are intrinsically rewarding for the child because they are designed to be fun. The games are created to capture each child's interest and imagination and to challenge the child's resources without frustrating them.

But sometimes extrinsic rewards, in the form of prizes, points, or tokens, are necessary to motivate the child's interest in the game. In these cases, the therapist is asking the child to give up long standing emotional and behavioral patterns, and even the most sensitively designed games will be met with some resistance. Earning tangible rewards or privileges can help motivate a child to face conflicts and challenges that he or she might otherwise avoid. Typically, points that are won in the game are converted to chips or some other token; these can then be cashed in for predetermined rewards.

THERAPEUTIC TECHNIQUES

To demonstrate how the developmental game technique can be used, I would like to take two case examples, one to show the process of designing a game, and the second to present the reader with an idea of how a series of developmental games might be used in an ongoing therapy.

A Neglected Learning-Disabled Boy Stops Running Away

Jay was an eight-year-old who had been tragically misplaced in institutions since the age of three. According to his social service record, he was placed in state custody shortly after his parent's separation. He was described as a "discipline problem" with moderate mental retardation (a misdiagnosis) and sent to a large public institution that had a reputation for its poor quality of care. No one paid attention to the fact that this child did not function like a retarded youngster, but rather as a child who suffered from neglect and specific developmental delays in several cognitive areas.

I saw Jay for the first time at the age of eight in an intermediate care facility where he had been placed as a step toward deinstitutionalization. When admitted, Jay appeared to be a sweet-natured boy, clearly suffering from his twin misfortunes of parental rejection and institutionalization. The staff was naturally shocked at the discrepancy between the child's appearance and his past history. There was the general feeling that Jay's stay at this facility would be a short one, and that he could soon be placed for adoption.

Hardly more than a week had passed before Jay began to exhibit a host of behavioral problems. He was belligerent to the staff and to the other children. He stole money, toys, food, almost anything that was of value to someone else. For a small boy, he had an incredible vocabulary of obscenities that he used to punctuate nearly every sentence. He was particularly troublesome in school where his difficulty in learning pre-academic skills was masked by these disruptive behaviors.

The most troubling problem of all was Jay's propensity for running away. Many children run away between the ages of seven and twelve. While they usually set out to express their anger and discontent, they also use this behavior as a metaphor for their growing sense of autonomy and their ambivalence about it. Running away from home, no matter how feeble the attempt, demonstrates the desire of children to test their limits for survival in the world. The proverbial peanut butter sandwich and bag of marbles in a knapsack is a symbolic gesture of children saying, "See, I don't need you! I can survive on my own," but at the same time, there is an equally strong wish to be proven wrong and yanked back into the nest. At this age children test themselves to see how far they can go, and they test their family's ability to make sure it isn't so far as to be unsafe.

However, in Jay's case, there appeared to be a different metaphor entirely. Jay's compulsive need to try and run away was not a gesture of a latency age child testing his independence, but rather that of a toddler being left out in the cold. Jay wasn't testing his inner resources, because he wasn't aware that he had any. He didn't need to see just how nurturant his environment would be, because his experience had told him that rather than stretching the tentacles of familial love, he would hardly be missed. In considering the meaning of his behavior, we must also recognize that Jay generally functioned two or three years below the eight years that his appearance suggested. Jay's concept of "home" must have meant only one thing to him, a place where he didn't belong.

The therapeutic game designed for Jay was called "Find Your Way Back Home." It consisted of a three-dimensional game board (see Figure 7 1) that used small toys to recreate the neighborhood around the facility where Jay was living. At the center of the game, there was a drawing of Jay's home at the facility with a small photo of Jay and his counselor placed inside. The game also included a small family of dolls (a mother, father, little boy, and little girl), who were used as the markers, and a spinner, with numbers 1 through 7 (as high as Jay could count).

The rules of the game were designed to create a situation where Jay would have to use a variety of new emotional, cognitive, and behavioral skills, as noted in the commentary below:

Rules For "Find Your Way Back Home" Game

Rules	Comments
1. Each player chooses one of the dolls to represent him/her in the game.	1. A family of dolls was chosen so that Jay would have an opportunity to express feelings about his family of origin. Often a "loaded" stimulus such as this will stimulate important play outside the game.

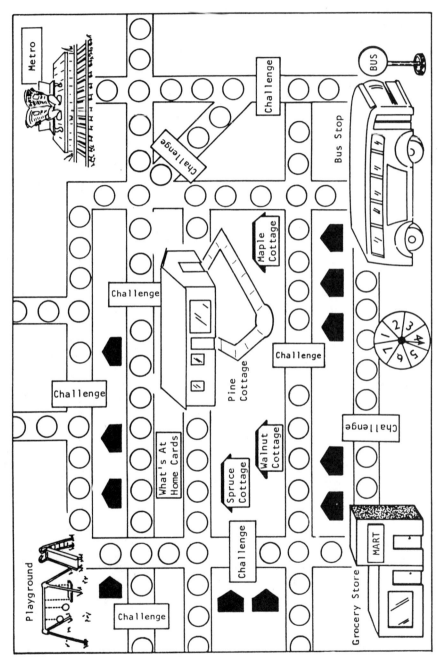

FIGURE 7.1. Plan for the "Find Your Way Home Game"

2. Each player spins the pointer and the highest number goes first.

2. Even the most basic rules can teach new skills. This rule introduces elementary concepts of cooperation, taking turns, and the "fairness" of chance.

3. The players can begin from any of the four corners: the metro station, the bus stop, the grocery store, or the playground.

3. The game begins with a choice, metaphorically an important one. In all choice situations, the therapist has an opportunity to model his/or thought processes and values (see the cognitive-mediating technique described in Chapter 5).

4. Taking turns, each player spins the pointer and advances in the direction of his/her choice, but each route eventually leads through the center (home) of the board. Unlike most board games there is no specific end point and the players can wander around the board indefinitely. The game ends when the players mutually decide that it should end. In spite of what the title implies, the sole object of the game is to explore the neighborhood and to learn new skills while doing so.

5. Throughout the "neighborhood" there are various squares that direct the player to take a "challenge" card. Each card describes a problem that the player must solve in order to win points.

6. The game is over when it is mutually decided by the players that they want to stop. At that time, each player may choose to "go home" and pick from a second set of cards labeled "What's At Home." On one side of each card is a description of something that is at home, and on the other side is the answer. If the correct answer is given, that player receives a ten point bonus.

6. It is taken for granted that the players go home after their adventures in the neighborhood, although this is not part of the rules, but a *choice* for each player. Since bonus points can be won by going "home," this is an added incentive to continue the metaphor.

Examples of "Challenge Cards"

"How much money does it take to ride the bus?"
"What do you do when you see a mean looking dog in someone's backyard?"
"What is the phone number of Mr. A (the counselor), if you get lost?"

Examples of "What's At Home Cards"

"Something's good for dinner. It used to go gobble, gobble, but now it just lies there in gravy."
"Who's thinking of you if it's past dinnertime and your seat is empty?"
"What's the largest picture you have in your room?"

Each time that Jay played the game, he had the opportunity to win points which would allow him to go on field trips with his therapist or his primary counselor. Although the game had no specific end-point, that is, no one won or lost, it was recommended that the playing time not be more than twenty minutes, for this was about the limit of Jay's attention span. During this time, it was anticipated that Jay would win between thirty and fifty points by solving the "Challenge" and "What's At Home Cards." He played the game every other day, either with his therapist who saw him twice a week, or with his counselor who was with him every day, giving Jay the opportunity to win one hundred to two hundred points a week. However, since Jay did not have these advanced number concepts, a pie with ten point slices that were colored in after every session was used to keep the cumulative score. When Jay won a specified number of points, he could trade them in for a trip to get a hamburger or ice cream, a movie, or another outing of his choice.

It is important to note that these trips were in no way contingent on Jay's improved behavior. Even if he ran away every day, he would still get his trip in the neighborhood when he won enough points. To withhold trips because Jay could not control his running away would have made him a prisoner in his own home, fueling his need to escape. Instead, contingencies for his running away were included in a separate behavioral program, which rewarded him with increased privileges in his cottage and punished him by removal of these privileges.

The "Finding Your Way Home Game" was played over a period of two months, and it was continually revised to meet Jay's changing needs and interests. With Jay's help, new Challenge cards, as well as new Home/Bonus cards, were made. The board was extended to include a downtown metro line that Jay wished to explore on the board as well as on his outings. Each change in the game gave the therapist a chance to learn more about Jay's way of thinking and interacting with the world, and this knowledge was then applied to the milieu treatment he received throughout the facility. For example, everyone who worked with Jay was given a 5 × 7 card with Jay's picture mounted on it. The card briefly and simply explained the nature of Jay's learning difficulty, and suggested optimum ways to communicate with him: "Speak slowly in simple sentences. Note if Jay is watching you and showing his understanding through his interests. Reinforce what you say with your own gestures. If it is important, ask Jay to repeat what he has heard. Be patient."

Jay stopped running away within the first two weeks of the program, but it is impossible to say whether this was due to added precautionary measures or to the treatment program. Because Jay's roaming around in the winter was so dangerous, the staff decided that they couldn't wait to see if the behavioral program would be effective, and a "reverse" burglar alarm system was installed in Jay's bedroom—a loud siren would go off if the windows or door were jarred. When Jay needed time alone, he spent it in his bedroom; at all other times he would be on a "buddy" system, where he would remain in sight of a counselor, teacher, or older resident. Running away or hiding from a buddy was used as the measure of the behavior we wished to extinguish; this decreased from an average of twice a day to twice a month by the end of the official treatment program.

MULTIPLE GAME THERAPY
WITH A HYPERACTIVE NINE YEAR OLD

From our first session together, it was clear that Ralph wouldn't like coming to psychotherapy. He much preferred playing ball with his friends or watching cartoons on T.V. to going to see a man about his problems. Fortunately Ralph did like to play games. Games could make him laugh, dance, reveal his thoughts and feelings, even sit down and work—quite an accomplishment for a boy whose special education teacher had described him as the most active child she had met in ten years of working with problem children.

Although Ralph had been somewhat calmed down from the medication prescribed by a pediatric neurologist for his attention span disorder and hyperactivity, he still had significant learning and behavioral problems. He was suspended from school at least once a month for infractions ranging from tardiness to provoking fist fights on the playground and stealing gum from his teacher's purse. His parents described him at home as a "happy-go-lucky kid," but one who was completely irresponsible. He would leave his chores after a few minutes, come home late for dinner, and carry out mischievous pranks that always seemed to border on being serious. Ralph's most significant problem in terms of its long term implications was his lack of motivation for school work. Academics were difficult for Ralph. Like many children who are diagnosed as hyperactive, he had an array of perceptual and cognitive deficits, but unlike many other learning disabled children, he had no heart for the struggle of learning and every semester fell further behind his appropriate grade level.

Looking back at his therapy, I think that I can honestly say that I did nothing but play games with Ralph, and since these games seemed to be beneficial, I had his teacher and parents play games as well.

Ralph's diagnostic assessment had suggested that his primary developmental problem was his lack of the establishment of an identity as a learner, a task that is normally accomplished by the time a child is in first grade. Ralph's four years of formal schooling had been filled with frustration and failure, and it was not surprising that he did not look to school to derive a sense of who he was and what he could do.

It was assumed that Ralph would acquire a sense of his ability to work and learn only when the adults in his life began to reflect back to him their recognition of his accomplishments. At a meeting to plan Ralph's treatment program, I asked each of his parents and his teachers what they thought Ralph would have to learn to become a better student at school and a more responsible child at home. Their replies: "He will have to learn to be on time." "He will have to learn to sit and work for at least a half an hour at a time." "He will have to start doing some chores around the house." "He will have to learn to obey rules."

Although I believed that all the adults in this conference sincerely cared for Ralph and wanted him to succeed, a certain defiance in their demands disturbed me. Ralph's diagnosis had made him something more than just a child—he was a *hyperactive child*. His disturbing behavior had defined him as an adversary to these adults, and I sensed that he must be changed, subdued, and defeated before he could be accepted. Another challenge from the adults in Ralph's life, directed at me, went something like: "I dare you to succeed where we have failed. He'll get you too, you'll see!" Such a double-bind, where there is resistance to have things change as well as to have them stay the same, is a common occurrence in child psychotherapy. Undoubtedly it involves forces which have contributed to and maintained the child's problem.

The developmental game technique can help redefine these adversarial roles, because it suggests that a child's emotional and behavioral problems reflect what he has learned and what he has failed to learn, not what he *is*. The importance of the therapist is de-emphasized, and the parents and other significant adults are realigned with the child as co-therapists. The idea of imposing change onto a child is replaced by structured experiences in the form of playful games, giving the child opportunities to develop in his own ways.

Over the course of four months, I introduced five games to Ralph, two of which I have included here. Many other games for over-active, impulsive children, can be found in *Games To Grow on: Activities to Help Children Learn Self-Control* (Shapiro, 1981).

Playing "Architect"

There are three major reasons why a school child has a hard time staying in his/her seat. First, he may have an organic predispostion toward excessive motor activity, and a short attention span. This can usually be controlled by dictary changes and/or appropriate medications. Then there is the factor of motivation. Crawling under a chair is more fun than sitting on it; if an active, curious child is not stimulated when he is seated, then ho will have a hard time repressing his urge to get up and seek things that interest him as he did when he was younger. The third reason, and perhaps the most overlooked, is that the seats themselves are uninviting. The mass produced seating found in our schools is made for the average child, but children who have difficulty learning and paying attention are not average. They often have highly developed senses that make them more reactive to their physical environment and body states, and at the same time they may lack the impulse control and other cognitive/affective traits that other children use to adapt to their environment.

In Ralph's case, his excessive motor activity had diminished as a result of medication and a change in his diet (which was free of sugar and artificial food additives). He was also fortunate enough to have a very creative teacher who individualized his curriculum so that it consisted of 70 to 80 percent high-interest material. But then there was the matter of his classroom chair, an old fashioned, wooden, ladderback that was more impressive for its durability than its comfort. I asked Ralph to play a game of "Architect" with me; he would be the architect, I would be the draftsman, and together we would make a chair that really suited him.

What makes a chair comfortable to sit in? Its height, its color, its padding, its shape, the fact that it can be wheeled around, recline, or even vibrate. Everyone has his/her own favorite place to sit and work, and kids are no exception—except that they rarely have a choice about where to sit or what to sit on.

When I asked Ralph what kind of chair he would like to sit in, he had no trouble making up his mind: "Oh, a rocketship chair that sits on the ground, with pictures of stars on it, and wings, and a real door to climb in, and instruments all over." When I asked him how this rocket-ship might be used for school work, he said, "It could have a little desk that folded down and compartments to keep my pencils and notebooks and stuff, and a cockpit light to shine on the books when I have to read so that I can see better." After another fifteen or twenty minutes discussing this contraption, we came up with a drawing similar to the one in Figure 7.2.

Thanks to the creativity and persistence of Ralph's mother and father and his teacher, Ms. M., Ralph's rocketship chair was launched in his classroom two weeks later. In fact, Ms. M. had opened the project to the other eight children in her special education classroom; within a few weeks the classroom contained more space ships, a racing car chair, a dinosaur chair, a cat, a dog, and a turtle chair, and a few free-form chairs that looked like creatures from another world. With the help of the

FIGURE 7.2. Ralph's Spaceship Chair

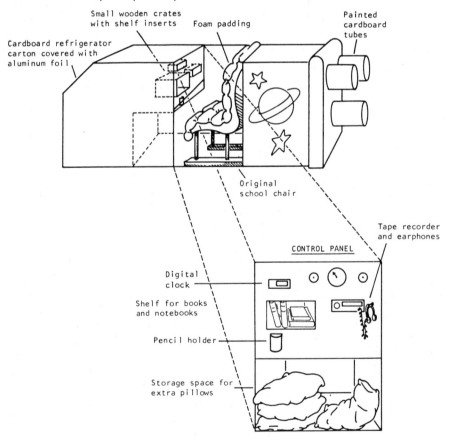

The Developmental Game Technique   119

school's art teacher and several parents, Ms. M. creatively combined the design and construction of her new seating with lessons in science, natural history, mathematics, and of course, reading. (For other examples of how specially designed classrooms can interest and motivate learning disabled children, see Sally Smith's book about the Kingsbury Lab School, NO EASY ANSWERS, 1979).

The Time On Your Hands Game

Another game that I introduced to Ralph involved a perpetual problem for both his parents and teachers—being on time. Like many learning disabled children Ralph had almost no sense of time and had great difficulty in reading a conventional clock. His parents had bought him watches, but he always lost them within a few days.

For this game I advised Ralph's parents to purchase a digital watch because they are easier for most learning disabled children to read. To Ralph's delight, they chose a "space cadet's" watch; to make sure it stayed around for awhile, I advised them to pin it each day to his shirt cuff or belt loop. After reviewing the basic time facts and making sure Ralph could read his new watch, we were ready to play.

The game began by drawing three pictures of the face of Ralph's watch and writing in the three times that it was most important for him to be punctual. The times selected by his parents were: 9:00 A.M., the time he had to be at his desk in school; 6 P.M., the time he had to be at home for dinner; and 9 P.M., the time he had to be in bed. Each of these pictures was then taped to an object near where Ralph had to be at that particular time—his desk at school (9 A.M.), the back of his chair at the dining room table (6 P.M.), and his bed post (9 P.M.). To win points, Ralph had to be at the right place at the exact time when the face on his watch matched the time shown on the drawing. Being early didn't count, since Ralph could then wander away and end up being late. Naturally an adult had to be at each point to check his punctuality and to give Ralph encouragement for his new found sense of time. Figure 7.3 shows the score sheet used to keep track of Ralph's progress.

As the people in Ralph's life began to play with him rather than criticize him and despair over his behavior, a subtle change began to appear in the way they talked about him and treated him. Where once his mother had greeted him after his therapy sessions with complaints and hard looks, she now began to greet him with smiles and hugs. His teacher reported that Ralph still had difficulties in class, but that he was a "happier child" who made friends more easily. Within a month after Ralph had started therapy, his school suspensions ceased, and he finished the year without any other further disciplinary action from the

Sequence No.	Counter Begin	No. End	Audio or Video Reference Begin	End
12	618	810	Alex walks in restaurant, says, "Hello, Guys"	Alex sits down at table; cut when he rests chin on hands
13	1003	1115	Pete says, "Whadda know, Buddy?"	Cut after close-up of Alex's smile
14	1301	1450	Alex says, "No thanks"	Alex sips his ginger ale. Add reinforcement here (dub in therapist's voice)

FIGURE 7.3. Score Sheet for Ralph's "Time on Your Hands Game"

principal. On his report card, Ralph had jumped from a "D" average to a "C plus."

When Ralph left therapy he had greatly improved on all our formal and informal measures . . . and all we did was play.

The Arts in Therapy

TYPES OF PROBLEMS

Autism; Childhood Schizophrenia; Depression; Hyperactivity; Learning Disabilities; Mental Retardation; Physical Handicaps; Psychosomatic Disorders and others.

Indicators

These techniques are particularly beneficial for children with multiple thinking, affective and behavioral disorders, and children with limited language or communication abilities. Each art modality also has its own specific indicators.

Contraindicators

There are no specific contraindicators for arts therapy techniques per se, but effective use of these techniques may require specialized training.

THERAPEUTIC PRINCIPLES AND TECHNIQUES

Art has been used as therapy since the beginnings of the human race and on up through the development of every civilization. Cave drawings from the late stages of the Stone Age suggest that art was used to treat physical and mental disorders; ancient Egyptian priest-physicians used chants as part of their healing process; the Greeks used dance as a "means of achieving health in every part of the individual" (Feder and Feder, 1981). From the inception of modern psychology, artwork has been used in the diagnosis of emotional problems, but it was not until the 1940s, with the writings of Margaret Naumberg, that art began to be recognized as a new form of therapy (Zwerling, 1979). Today the arts are valued as potent tools in the treatment of both childhood and adult disorders.

The actual use of the arts in therapy has developed in several different directions and has raised many questions as to how these techniques should be applied, in what context, and by whom. Initially mainstream psychiatry saw art techniques as adjunctive to traditional treatment or solely as a diagnostic tool. However, creative arts therapists are now trained to use the various art modalities as a primary treatment. Dr. Israel Zwerling of the Hahnemann Medical College in Philadelphia is an advocate from the field of psychiatry who strongly and articulately asserts that creative arts therapists have the credentials to be recognized as therapists in their own right with a unique contribution to the treatment process. He notes that the training of arts therapists includes theory and practical experience in all the basic and applied areas of psychology, including "personality theory, psychopathology, psychodynamics, and individual family and group psychotherapy—in addition to the content related to the application of (their) particular creative art form (Zwerling, 1979)." Like other therapists, he continues, creative arts therapists base their treatment on thorough diagnostic procedures, a flexible and empathic relationship to the patient, and the confrontation of specific dysfunctional symptoms as well as the broader goal of personality growth and development.

In direct contrast, there are those who argue that professional training is antithetical to art and that only artists themselves can effectively tap the creative energies of problem children. An example of this approach is the Living Stage Theater in Washington, D.C., a nationally recognized improvisational company working with severely disabled children, including the retarded and physically handicapped, the deaf, the blind, and imprisoned delinquents. The company uses song, dance, and poetry to encourage self-expression and self-worth.

Another approach to the therapeutic use of art with children emphasizes the role of art in the educational process. Sally Smith, director of the Kingsbury Lab School in Washington, D.C., has designed a curriculum with arts at its core for her unique school for learning disabled children. As she states in her book *No Easy Answers:*

> I not only believe in the intrinsic value of the arts to better the human condition, but also that children love to participate in most of the arts. They become totally involved. Further, the arts provide activity learning, and immature children need a great deal of this type of learning to gain that total involvement and to ensure their understanding of the material. The arts lend themselves to the imaginative use of concrete materials and experiences to teach abstract ideas. Neural immaturity makes it very hard for the learning disabled child to grasp abstractions. He has to be introduced to them through his body, through objects and pictures, and then through symbols. The arts offer opportunities to strengthen visual, auditory, tactile, and motor areas. Through the arts, a child can order his world, make sense of what he knows, relate past experience to the present, and turn muscular activity into thought and ideas into action. (Smith, 1981)

Although there is a controversy in how art can most effectively be used to help children with problems, my guidelines for choosing art techniques follows the recommendations made in Chapter 2 on choosing any method of treatment:

a) Choose the specific art modality on the basis of thorough and appropriate diagnostic assessments of the child, including the use of the arts themselves.

b) Use techniques that address the child's strengths and weaknesses and direct them to both the presenting problem as well as to the underlying developmental and personality issues.

c) Don't go beyond the limits of your professional expertise and make appropriate referrals when necessary. If referrals are made, all professionals seeing the child should communicate closely and work toward the same goals and objectives.

d) Evaluate the success of each technique with objective data to assure its effectiveness and progression toward the defined criteria for success.

The techniques in this chapter are presented in the order of developmental issues. "Writing" techniques generally assume the highest level of development, not being appropriate for children with developmental skills of less than eight or nine years. Arts in education is presented next, since these techniques are typically used to teach basic academic and pre-academic skills for children age 5 and up. Except when used as a tool for simple catharsis, visual arts techniques assume an ability for symbolization outside the body, which occurs at approximately two years. Music and dance/movement therapy are presented last because they can address the pre-verbal and pre-symbolic developmental issues based in infancy.

Writing As Therapy

Like other art techniques, writing can serve several diverse therapeutic functions. Diagnostically it can give insight into a child's or adolescent's cognitive structures, use of language, verbal fluency, imagination, and even style of personality. Writing can help articulate feelings, images, and vague thoughts that might otherwise remain out of the child's conscious awareness. It can break through inhibitions that might be present in verbal conversations with an adult, and it can add a new dimension to the therapy as a tool for self-awareness and interpersonal communication.

When I use writing as a part of a multiple-technique treatment program, it must originate with the interest of the child or adolescent. Writing is often perceived as "work" by students, and I am not interested in being cast in the role of another teacher. I usually let the offer to write come from the client himself. Such was the case with Allen, an adolescent who had been diagnosed as a borderline personality with obsessive/compulsive character traits.

I worked with Allen when I was employed by a psychoanalytically oriented school for emotionally disturbed adolescents. Although many of the students had idiosyncratic behaviors and mannerisms, Allen seemed intent on standing out from the crowd. Allen had many obsessions and compulsive rituals that he liked to talk about because people found them strangely amusing and accepted Allen as an eccentric. One of his most complex and frequent obsessions was about the New York City subway system. Allen had memorized the entire subway schedule for all the boroughs. Not only could he tell you which trains stopped at which stations, but he knew where they all connected, which lines had the newest cars and the best efficiency ratings, where muggings were most likely to occur, and so on. He frequently rode the subways for hours on end to verify his wealth of facts. At least one time when he decided to run away from home, he road the subway all night for twelve straight hours.

When Allen talked about the subways, it was in excited run-on sentences, in the manner of an announcer at a racetrack. Once I overheard another student ask him for directions to a place in Queens. Although I couldn't really follow what Allen said, not being very familiar with the system myself, this is how Allen's reply sounded to me: "You want to get to Flatbush Avenue? Great. I'll get you there in twenty-two and a half minutes. Now, first walk down to Ninety-Second Street, and take the IRT down to Forty-Second. Then switch to the AA and go down to Sixth Avenue. That is, unless it's between four and seven o'clock, and then I want you to take the No. 6 down to Wall Street and change to the No. 8. Now you have to run very fast to the Express and hop on three stops if it's exactly fifteen minutes after the hour and four stops if it's thirty past the hour, and then take the B train three stops and you'll be there. Of course if you're traveling in the morning, or you miss the No. 6 at Forty-Second, then . . ."

When I saw Allen in therapy, I discouraged him from talking about his obsessions, assuming that he used them as a magical shield to protect his real, but fragile self. This was very disappointing to Allen, but he seemed to respect the legitimacy of my decision. He asked, however, if he could keep a journal of the obsessions and rituals that I didn't want to hear about. This seemed like an odd request to me at the time, but no odder than the obsessions themselves. I saw Allen twice a week, and generally talked to him about a broad range of subjects building on our relationship rather than trying to uncover some deep unconscious conflicts (see reality therapy, Chapter 3). At the end of each session, Allen would hand me his journal, and I would read it and return it to him with comments by the end of the day. Allen wrote primarily about his obsessions and compulsive rituals. He wrote about the Jewish dietary laws; about how he washed his hair; about the state of the art of New York pretzels . . . all with the same excited and associative manner he used when he talked about subways. Then after about a month of this he also wrote a poem: "My life is like a loaf of bread/ Everyone takes a slice./

Some butter me up but good, others put me in a jam./ I hope they don't let me go stale." This short poem was a major breakthrough. For the first time, Allen had found a metaphor for his feelings other than his obsessive detailing and compulsive rituals. I interpreted the metaphor as Allen saying that he saw himself only in parts, parts manufactured for the tastes and pleasures of others. While some people responded to his "parts" by "buttering him up," others had no use for him and he was in danger of going stale. I further assumed that Allen's obsessions and compulsions had something to do with this view of himself. Since Allen seemed so eager to communicate about his elaborate thought schemes and rituals, I hypothesized that each one was devised for both intrapsychic and interpersonal reasons. I wondered if Allen chose certain obsessions to communicate with certain people. Some were meant to please, some were meant to anger and frustrate, all were meant to keep people at just the distance Allen wanted. Similarly, his compulsions that were exclusively carried out at home were ways to express his feelings toward his parents. The hair washing ritual that occurred every morning and every night kept him in the shower for forty-five minutes at a time, precisely at periods of the day when his parents might also want to use the only bathroom in the apartment.

Of course, all of this was conjecture. Each hypothesis would have to be tested out slowly in the context of a relationship based on acceptance of Allen as a whole person and the presentation of myself in the same way. I answered Allen's poem using the same metaphor, trying to recreate his irony and humor: "I like bread and butter/ It's nourishing and delish/ I'd rather spend an hour with a loaf of bread/ then spend all day with a brussel sprout."

As the weeks went by, Allen slowly stopped writing about his obsessive thoughts and ritualistic behaviors. We found many ways to communicate through his journal: word games, pictures, short stories, and more poems. As a result of continued individual treatment, the milieu therapy of the school, and family therapy, Allen was able to move out of his home and attend college on a part-time basis the following year.

The Arts In Education

The importance of using arts and art therapies in education has been recognized in federal legislation. Public Law 94-142, the Education for All Handicapped Children's Act, was passed by Congress in the mid 1970s to insure that all children with disabilities would have access to the appropriate services they needed to fulfill their learning potential. Public Law 94-142 specifically mentioned the appropriateness of using art and art therapies in the education of children with special needs. Although the spirit of this law was widely praised and at the time seen as a "coming of age" for the application of mental health principles to public education, its implementation has in many ways fallen short of the expectations of special educators and the hopes of parents, children, and therapists in the schools. Ambiguities in the law itself, the widely varying perspectives of school boards across the country, changes in the structure of the federal bureaucracy, and most of all the realization of how expensive this program would be, have held back the dramatic changes that many of us had hoped for in the education of the handicapped.

Still, some progress has been made, particulary in the private sector where government support in the form of tuition grants for handicapped children has encouraged creative educational experiments. One such program that has already been mentioned is the Kingsbury Lab School directed by Sally Smith. Ms. Smith, the mother of a significantly learning disabled child who did not read until he was thirteen, has won national recognition for her school. The school has worked with hundreds of severely handicapped children and ninety percent of her students return to regular classroom settings. Many have gone on to college. The curriculum at the Lab School is built around the arts. Half the day is spent in the classroom, and the other half is spent in woodwork, music, dance, drama, puppetry, and filmmaking. Ms. Smith sees the artist/ teacher as contributing to every phase of the child's treatment. Difficulties that the child has in an art medium provide important diagnostic information about the way that the child thinks and perceives. Attention to the art forms that the students excel at provides information about what each child needs to learn to succeed in academics.

The inherent structure in each of the arts and the ability of artists to see the world in a purposeful organized way are the keys to using art to teach the learning disabled child. Labelling, discriminating, sorting, comparing, grouping, classifying, synthesizing, preparing, and planning are the basic building blocks of all learning. The arts provide the opportunities for children to experience all of these cognitive processes at whatever developmental level they are on, while holding their interest and motivating them to muster their resources in ways that traditional academic teaching doesn't seem able to do.

Several years ago I worked with a ten-year-old with a learning disability that prevented him from learning mathematics beyond a first-grade level, even though he performed at an above average level in many of the areas we associate with "intelligence." His vocabulary, his memory for details, and his skill at solving visual puzzles all suggested that he should have been able to perform at least as well as other children his age if not better. Still, numbers didn't make sense for him and he avoided anything resembling math problems so he wouldn't appear and feel stupid. But this same boy was also enrolled in a film-making workshop. Each member of the class had been asked to make a ten-minute film about any subject, and he had chosen his passion—electronic games. His film teacher asked him what the film would be about, and he replied that some adults thought that electronic games were dumb and even bad for kids, and he wanted to show them that games are worthwhile not only because kids love to play them, but also because they can help kids learn as well.

Before the project had even begun, the relationship of the teacher to the student had been defined in terms of the child's interests and emotional needs. Art, unlike traditional education, does not impose values on the child, and so he is free to choose a subject that makes him feel good about himself and a message that affirms his pride in his achievements rather than his shame about his disability. The next step was to channel his interest so that it could include instruction in basic skills.

The teacher began by explaining how the student must organize his "film" on paper before he began to use the camera. He suggested that a story board of the film should be made by drawing a sketch of each scene, noting how many minutes each shot should take, and arranging them in a sequence that most effectively tells the message. He gave the student a film book showing how a story board was made for a popular adventure movie. He reminded him that each student only had a limited amount of film to work with, the equivalent of twenty minutes, and that the edited version should be about five minutes in length. Now here is a complicated mathematical problem for a child who has trouble with simple subtraction, so the boy took the task to his math teacher for help. Although theoretically the math involved was well beyond the child's level, involving the division of the total number of minutes of filming by the number of scenes, the film teacher had successfully concretized and organized the task so that the math teacher could then break it down into manageable steps. The boy had decided that he wanted to shoot five scenes: one of a video-arcade; one showing two friends playing a hand-held game; one showing a child beating an adult at the same game; a fourth showing an interview of the science teacher explaining the relationship between electronic games and computers; and the fifth showing himself working at a computer. The student made one sketch for each scene. Then, the math teacher took a large piece of poster board measuring exactly twenty inches across and drew a straight line at the top. She explained that the board that would hold the sketches was exactly twenty inches wide and asked the student to take a yardstick and make a mark for each inch. When this was done, she explained that each mark would represent a minute of filming and had him number the marks up to twenty. She then asked the student to make three sets of five cards each: one set was to be three inches square, another, four inches square, and the last, five inches square. She also had him mark out the top of each card in inches. She then explained the principle of division, the meaning of dividends and divisors, the symbol for division, and so forth. She knew that she was only introducing these concepts and did not imply that they should be mastered just yet. But she also let the student know that these concepts were the basic elements of his problem and were exactly what other kids of his age were learning.

She then asked him to take each set of five cards and to see which fit exactly on the story board. Only one would fit, she explained, and the number of inches on the top of those cards would indicate the number of minutes that he could film each scene. She then directed the student to take the cards that fit the story board and paste his sketches on them. Finally, she sent him back to the film teacher with the equipment for the story board completed. He could now discuss the best sequence for his scenes to convey his message.

Let's review what happened. A child with no interest in math, who normally performed three years below his age level, excitedly solved a math problem at an age appropriate level by having it broken down into concrete tasks that he could master. In doing so, he performed operations in measuring, in equating different systems of measurement (that is, inches and minutes), in sequencing, in comparison, in numbering, and so on. In addition, he was introduced to the basic principles behind a mathematical concept presumed to be far out of his reach. Since the same basic task would be repeated several more times before the actual filming got underway (scenes would have to be divided into "shots," dialogue would have to be added, and so forth), the student had the opportunity to repeat the process over and over again, strengthening each of the basic organizational tasks he had to learn. But most important, this child found repeated success, strengthening his belief in his own powers to learn, and motivating him toward continued progress.

The remainder of this chapter is devoted to the creative arts therapies of visual art, music, and dance/movement. Although these are three distinct therapies, each with its own history of development, methodologies, and professional organizations, many creative arts therapists have been trained in the use of all three modalities and may use considerable crossover in their work. While some of the techniques I will discuss may be appropriate for use by therapists not specifically trained in the creative arts, others remain in the province of those with a degree in this field. Obviously, it is in the best interest of all to find the most qualified practitioners available and to make referrals or work conjointly as dictated by the needs of the client.

Visual Art Therapy

Visual art therapy, usually referred to as art therapy, will be the first of the creative arts therapies to be discussed. Drawings are frequently used by "mainstream" psychotherapists (therapists without specific training in art therapy) as part of their diagnostic assessments of children. Common methods for using drawings to assess the personality makeup and conflicts of children include the Human Figure Drawing Test (Koppitz, 1968), the House-Tree-Person Test, and the Kinetic Family Drawing (Burns and Kaufman, 1970). Although considerable controversy exists about the validity of each of these techniques to add to a differential diagnosis, the ease of their use and the richness of their product continues to assure their popularity. Each technique begins with a simple direction:

> Human Figure Drawing: "Draw a person for me on this sheet of paper."
> "Now draw a picture of a boy/girl (the opposite sex of the first drawing) on the back."
> House-Tree-Person Test: "Draw me a picture of a house, a tree, and a person, using this pencil." "Now draw me another picture of a house, a tree, and a person, using these crayons."
> Kinetic Family Drawing: 'Draw me a picture of your family doing something."

Directions may vary slightly, but all advocates of these techniques emphasize to the child that the artistic quality of the drawings is not important and that anything they produce is of value. The drawings are then interpreted by the following: specific symbols that the child uses (although interpreting a one-to-one correspondence between a symbol in a drawing and a universal meaning is frowned upon); the way that the child uses the writing instruments and the paper; the degree of tension exhibited by the lightness or width of the line; the spacing of the drawing(s) on the page; the use of color in the House-Tree-Person test; the exaggeration of specific features (particularly in the body) and the absence of others; and in the Kinetic Family Drawing, the choice of activity, relative size of the family members, the style of the drawings, and so forth.

Although as Feder and Feder suggest (1981), the diagnostic use of art cannot really be separated from its theapeutic use, but there are specific functions of visual art techniques which designate this modality as a distinct therapy. They note that while there is a wide variation in the use of art therapy, the majority of art therapists come from a Freudian or neo-Freudian tradition, and define the benefits of art therapy in psychodynamic concepts. In this framework, the most basic benefits to be gained by art therapy are through cartharsis, the release of emotional energy and tension. Clay, fingerpaints, play dough, water, and sand have always been standard equipment in the analytic playroom to promote the free expression of pent-up conflicts and inhibitions. The choice of materials, colors, the manner in which these are used, and the verbalizations that accompany their use provide clues as to where a child's unconscious anxieties may be located and the particular ego-defense structures that may be either restricting or failing to bind the libidinal or aggressive drives.

A second function of art therapy is to provide a channel between the patient's conscious and unconscious mind. Within this concept, art may be seen as a sublimation of unconscious drives and conflicts, a symbolization of unconscious images such as we find in dreams, or an integration of thoughts, feelings, and behaviors, both conscious and unconscious, that leads to a sense of fulfillment as a "whole person" in the process of creating art.

The most important contribution of art to the therapeutic process, however, may be its capacity to act as a channel of non-verbal communication. As in the related creative art therapies of music and dance, the possibilities for communicating outside the limitations of words can open up new vistas to the patient and the therapeutic relationship. Through their artistic creations patients can explore issues that have been so emotionally laden that they have been prohibited from finding conscious verbal expression, or issues that are so basic in their origin in the first years of life that they predate the child's ability to use words. An example of this communicative use of art occurred in a family session where I was a co-therapist with an analytic colleague. The identified patient was a four-year-old boy who had an older brother with a severe hearing loss and concomitant speech and language problems.

Since birth the younger boy, Mark, had been relegated to the role of the "normal" child by the parents, whose marriage had nearly broken up over the difficulties in raising their older handicapped son. Now the younger boy was beginning to display his own set of serious problems. In the six months before they sought therapy, Mark had become increasingly belligerent toward his older brother as well as toward children his own age. He verbally and physically teased them and also expressed violent fantasies when he was the least bit annoyed. His mother reported a recent incident that had occurred while Mark was riding with several other children to preschool. Another child had inadvertently bumped his shoulder, and Mark had turned in a rage and said, "I'm going to kill you for that, I'm going to take my Daddy's gun and shoot you in the head until you bleed and you're dead."

As could have been anticipated, Mark's behavior once again threw the family into disarray. Both the mother and father felt that they had somehow been cursed to bring up children who would be outcasts of society.

In the fourth conjoint family session an incident occurred that demonstrated how an art technique can be used both in a psycho-dynamic and a family framework. I was talking to the mother and father who were seated at opposite ends of the couch, when my colleague noticed a drawing that Mark was doing in a corner of the room. The older boy was sitting in a chair close to his mother's end of the couch. I always keep drawing and other art materials available during family sessions, but this was the first time that Mark had used them. Immediately prior to selecting some paper and a box of crayons he had been jumping on and off the couch in between his parents until his mother angrily told him to "stop it." When my co-therapist observed that Mark had completed his drawing, she asked him if he would bring it over to show her (she was positioned in the center of the room) and to also bring some paper and the box of crayons. Mark's drawing showed four stick figures—three of about equal size in the middle of the page and one much smaller lying on its back in the corner. When Mark was asked who these people were, he indicated that he was in the center of the picture, sandwiched between his mother and father, and his older brother was in the corner. When he was asked what the people were doing, he replied that he and his Mommy and Daddy were talking, and his older brother was going to his "special" school. My colleague replied that she liked the picture and she understood how children often wished to have their Mommies and Daddies all to themselves and not have to share them with anyone. She went on: "This is a wish that most children have, but it is only a wish. Even babies don't get their parents all to themselves. Parents must have time for each other and for other children in the family." Mark and the rest of the family listened to this quietly. Mark was fiddling with the crayons and my colleague asked him if he wanted to color his picture in, but he replied, "No." (We assumed that this was because he was not yet ready to deal with emotional colorations of what he had just revealed. Note that his story expressed none of his anger toward his older sibling, even though the prone positioning of the smaller figure suggested that the impulse was there.)

I then suggested that it would be interesting to see some more pictures of the family. I gave a new sheet of paper to Mark and to his brother, and asked the parents if they would draw a picture together on a single sheet of paper. I asked them to move together on the couch and gave them a clipboard and a box of crayons. My colleague and I positioned ourselves on either side of the two children, who were now seated much farther from the couch. Each child had his own box of crayons.

In the remainder of the session we used the pictures as a stimulus to talk about each person's wishes about "the way the family could be." In each case, the therapists recognized the legitimacy of the fantasies and talked about some of the other ways besides wishing that children and adults can fulfill their needs. The session ended with an assignment for the family to go home and do a joint poster showing everyone in the family doing what he/she likes best. Specific directions were given to the parents on how to structure the task, how to intervene if the children began to fight, and how to set the limits on the task.

Music Therapy

Although music therapy initially grew from a more behavioral model than the other arts therapies, its application to the treatment of children has more recently been influenced by the developmental point of view. The developmental significance of music therapy goes back before the child is born to the prenatal influences of the mother's and child's heartbeats and the intrauterine vibrations and rhythms. During the first year of life there is a rich interchange of nonverbal "music" between the infant and his/her environment as the infant begins to cry, coo, hum, babble, and respond to the parents. By the second year of life words are added to the child's vocalizations and soon simple song patterns are put together (Levick et al., 1979). While many of the songs of early childhood are used to teach basic cognitive concepts ("One, two, buckle my shoe . . .") or to stimulate the child's motor coordination ("Patty Cake, Patty Cake, Baker's Man . . .") the primary function of these musical experiences is to augment the pleasurable bond between adult and child and to communicate on an emotional level.

Since both music and dance/movement therapy often utilize pre-verbal psychological parameters, it is sometimes arbitrary to define a boundary where one modality stops and the other begins. For this reason it is common for music and dance/movement therapists to use some of the same treatment methods.

The ability of creative arts therapists to cross over from one modality to another was demonstrated by a colleague of mine at a treatment center for handicapped children. Shawn, a ten-year-old moderately retarded boy with a severe language deficit, had been a resident of the center for several years and had made consistent but slow progress with various therapy and educational approaches during most of that time. Although his speech consisted of one- or two-word phrases and echolalic repetitions of his teachers and counselors, Shawn also had begun to use sign language as a means of communication and could express himself on a three year level. Shawn's world suddenly seemed to fall apart, however, when his parents announced that they were going to separate. Even though he had not lived at home for several years, the conflict and anxiety that his parents generated in their frequent visits had a dramatic effect. Once an affable and outgoing child, Shawn suddenly became sullen and depressed. He rarely spoke, his appetite diminished, he slept more than normal, and he showed no interest at all in learning.

Although there were many people with whom Shawn had close relationships, including teachers, counselors, and his speech therapist, no one knew how to approach him now. Without a formal language to express himself, Shawn suddenly seemed to be enclosed in a glass case. The people who cared for him could look in and observe, but they couldn't get through.

Shawn was referred for dance/movement therapy in the hope that a therapy that did not rely on words would aid Shawn in expressing his emotional troubles. Therapy was begun with a nonverbal developmental assessment (described in the next section) to determine a developmenal profile and to get a sense of which modalities Shawn might be responsive to. His therapist noted that Shawn seemed to enjoy the opportunities to dance and move, during which he sang a melodic and rhythmic series of sounds. This was a common behavior of Shawn's which other adults heard as a self-stimulating monologue common to many non-verbal retardates. But his therapist began to see this song as a way of communicating. She listened to Shawn's "singing" and sang back. He was delighted and began to see this mirroring as it was intended—a valuing and acceptance of who he was, and the beginning of a dialogue that became an integral part of treating his depression.

Similar examples of the use of music as an entree to the closed world of the nonverbal retarded or autistic child can be found throughout the case reports of music therapists. Children who have never smiled light up when they hear a rhythm they have tapped on a drum being repeated. Children who have spent years of their lives on back wards twiddling their fingers and manipulating the same objects have learned to say "hello" by a particular strum on a guitar, or "I'm angry" by the crash of a cymbal. Participation in a rhythm band might be the first interaction these children have ever had with others their own age, and their response to simple repetitive songs might be their first indication of a willingness to listen and learn.

In Shawn's case, his therapist found that his vocalizations increased in their range and complexity as the sessions went on. Movement to accompany Shawn's vocalizations was added to further enlarge his new affective language. At the same time his therapist verbally acknowledged what he expressed: "You're going up, up, up! Strong, tall Shawn! Now, down, down, down!"

Although music therapy has made some important contributions to working with severely handicapped, non-verbal patients, these children are by no means the only types of children who can benefit from it. Music is intertwined throughout the lives of all children and has a particular interest and meaning for children who might otherwise be impossible to reach. I was recently asked by a private school to suggest a treatment for a nine-year-old boy named Jacob who had been placed in a class for learning disabled children with behavioral problems. Jacob had created a role for himself as the class clown; in a class of rambunctious, rebellious boys, establishing this role takes some doing. Whatever the teacher asked of Jacob, he did the opposite. If she wanted him to raise his hand to be called on, he insisted on calling out. If she wanted him to ask permission to leave the room, he simply got up and did as he pleased. What really drove his teacher nuts was Jacob's constant tapping. He tapped with his pencil, with his fingers, and with his feet. Sometimes he did it deliberately to fluster and interrupt Ms. B., but many other times he tapped for the sheer enjoyment of the rhythm.

Jacob and his teacher battled every day, but although he smiled and laughed when he thought he had gotten away with something, he was far from being happy. He lived at home with his mother and a baby brother and, from his teacher's account, he was virtually ignored. Court proceedings were in progress to remove Jacob from his home due to parental neglect and to place him in a foster home. Even at school, where he tried so hard to be accepted by his schoolmates, his lack of progress in learning made him feel like an outcast. A token economy program that his teacher had instigated at the beginning of school made it clear that while Jacob enjoyed clowning around, there was not much in it for him except a few laughs from his buddies. When the tokens were cashed in at the end of each week, Jacob rarely had any to show, and he was unable to purchase the treats or special privileges.

When I saw Jacob by himself, he showed none of the recalcitrant behaviors that his teacher had described, but on the other hand, he was not thrilled to be seeing me. I questioned him about his interests and hobbies, deliberately trying to avoid topics that might make him more defensive, but he showed little interest in my attempts at conversation. Being circumspect wasn't getting me very far, so I decided to be blunt:

THERAPIST: Well, I guess you know why you're down here seeing me, don't you? Ms. B. says that you're not very happy about being in her class and she's not very happy about all the trouble you give her.
JACOB: Yup. I know.
THERAPIST: And she thinks that I might have some ideas to turn the situation around.
JACOB: Humph.
THERAPIST: Do you know what you do that really bugs the hell out of her?
JACOB: (interested) No . . . what?
THERAPIST: This! (I tap out a complicated beat.)
JACOB: (giggles) Oh, that!
THERAPIST: Yup. This! (Another rhythm.)
JACOB: (smiling) You mean this? (He beats out about 30 seconds of a syncopated beat.)
THERAPIST: That's it! (I repeat the rhythm.)

We went on like this, beating out rhythms back and forth like a drum duel between two hot-shot drummers in rival bands. Although the mood was competitive, there was also a feeling of mutual respect. We got into a pattern of copying each other's beat and then adding another flourish. When I couldn't quite get the rhythm that Jacob had given me, or vice versa, we showed each other how to do it. We kept this up for the remainder of the session, and at the end of our time, I said, "See you next week," and beat out the rhythm of the words. Jacob did the same.

After that session, I wondered whether the behavior that so annoyed Ms. B. could be used as a bridge between her and Jacob. Jacob's tapping had always been termed disruptive, but it was also something he enjoyed and obviously could communicate with. The next week, after greeting Jacob with a tapped message, I asked if he might be interested in learning to use his taps in the classroom in a way that Ms. B. would accept. He looked at me suspiciously. I then talked to him about the Morse Code, about the ways that American Indians used to send messages by drumbeats, and about the way blind people use their canes to tap the ground to determine what's ahead or if there are obstacles in the way. I told him that we could make up our own tapping code to help him communicate with Ms. B. in ways that would suit both of them, and that would help him earn some of the tokens that he was missing out on in class. I asked Jacob three things that he thought Ms. B. would like him to be able to say to her. He offered: "Can I sharpen my pencil?" "Can I go to the bathroom?" and "I need help." We worked out a system of rhythmic taps that seemed to fit these phrases and that afternoon I presented them to Ms. B. She readily agreed that she would try anything. We decided that Jacob could earn points from the class's token economy every time he appropriately communicated with his taps. He would get points taken away, however, if he tapped on his desk inappropriately. At the same time, as part of a multiple technique treatment plan, I suggested several other techniques for Ms. B. to use in the classroom and made an immediate referral to a music therapist.

Dance/Movement Therapy

Although the relationship of the mind to the body has interested modern psychotherapists since Freud's early work with hysteria, it has taken the field of dance/movement therapy to develop a systematic approach, integrating traditional psychological schools of thought (most notably developmental, psychodynamic and systems theory) with a new understanding of body movement and the language of nonverbal communication. While other schools of therapy have expressed interest in body tension, position, and posture, dance/movement therapy is the only one stressing the developmental significance of movement and the ever present context of nonverbal interaction as an integral part of therapy and potent catalyst of change.

Human movement can be classified in many ways. Among several notational systems that have developed to describe the complex, uniquely patterned series of changes which comprise even our most mundane actions, Effort-Shape is most widely used in assessment, diagnosis, and treatment. Developed in the 1940s by Rudolf Laban, Effort-Shape is a system that describes the qualitative aspects of movement, analyzing how we move in relation to space, weight, time, and flow.

The analysis of movement and its implications for treatment is probably the most difficult of the various creative arts therapy techniques for a traditionally-trained psychotherapist to understand. Part of the difficulty is the paradox of using words to describe what is nonverbal. The language of Effort-Shape is meant to take us beyond our traditional ways of thinking:

> From a piece of music we can isolate and study the dynamics of pitch, tone, rhythm, and amplitude; or we can look at its structure as a composition of notes, a key signature, and phrasing. Seeing a tapestry, our eye may go to a particular color or texture, following the ins and outs from one side to the other. If we wanted to understand the experience of playing the music or weaving the tapestry, and to know by more than one sensory faculty all the elements of their composition, we would have to analyze all the component parts and perhaps actually play the

piece and weave a replica. In Effort-Shape analysis, we essentially do both: the accuracy of our observations is contingent upon our ability to replicate and experience bodily the qualitative changes in form and effort which we perceive. So we are describing at once what is happening and how it feels. The individual uniqueness and integrity of the object of description emerges in the form of movement patterns which appear with consistency. From field glasses to magnifying lens we switch, and back again; shifting of figure and ground proceed until the complex whole becomes apparent. (Lamb, 1979)

Briefly, the major concepts in Effort-Shape analysis include:

Effort Flow.   The basic energy of body movement. An everpresent quality of liveliness along a continuum of restraint (bound flow) to ease of control (free flow).

Shape Flow.   The movement of one or more body part(s) in its adaptation to space.

Kinesphere.   The space around the body that can be reached while one foot remains in place.

Weight.   The active relationship of the body in relationship to gravity on a continuum from light (buoyant) to strong (forceful).

Space.   The manner in which a person approaches his/her environment on a continuum from indirect (multi-focused) to direct (tunnel vision).

Time.   The way in which a person uses time to perform specific activities ranging from quick (abrupt) to sustained (leisurely).

Planes.   The three basic planes of movement are vertical (as in standing upright or jumping rope), horizontal (as in dinner-table behavior), and saggital (as in doing somersaults).
        Each of the efforts and planes emerge with predominant elements and combinations at different ages; these in turn roughly correspond to the developmental tasks associated with those ages. For example, the infant (0 to age one) generally moves in a horizontal plane with the predominating effort of flow varying from bound to free; these qualities assist in the developmental tasks of attunement, communication, and object constancy accomplished in the progressive duet or synchronous interplay between parent and child. The toddler generally moves in the vertical plane with weight as the predominant effort,

corresponding to the developmental tasks of separation and individuation. By the time the child is of school age (three and one-half to five) all planes and all efforts are used, although there is a particular emphasis on the efforts of time, and the use of space becomes more defined during this period.

The developmental schema of movement analysis is particularly relevant to the treatment of nonverbal children who have been ignored by the vast majority of psychological tests and techniques. A movement analysis of a child would look at what Effort-Shape elements predominate, which ones are missing, how they are integrated, and how they relate particular sets of problems. A few brief observations of a child spontaneously at play, in class, and/or with the family can yield a wealth of data that can be used to pinpoint specific strengths, weaknesses, developmental deficiencies, and possible directions for treatment.

Most autistic children have a very limited repertoire of movement. They may rigidly adhere either to a vertical plane, walking and sitting stiffly like robots, or to a horizontal plane, preferring to lie on their stomachs or backs and cutting out stimulation from the world around them. Meeting such a child on the developmental body level can create the possibility of communication with another human being, and thus a means to grow, and conversely, ignoring the non-verbal language of children can serve to strengthen the walls they build around themselves.

I recall a time when I was walking by the physical therapy room in a center for multi-handicapped children where I worked. I had stopped short at the sound of the most pathetic crying and wailing. As I opened the door, I anticipated seeing a child being beaten, only to find the physical therapist innocently coaxing an autistic five-year-old to try and balance on a large foam ball. The physical therapist couldn't understand the child's distress. She explained that she was trying to get the little girl to stop walking on her toes (a characteristic of many autistic children) by placing her on a ball where she would have to move from heel to toe and back to keep from falling off. Even though the physical therapist had a firm grip on her and was obviously not going to let the child fall, the little girl's reaction was as if she were being forced over a cliff. Still, the physical therapist persisted, determined to "help" her. By a fortunate coincidence, the dance/movement therapist was also walking by at the time and immediately recognized the screams of one of her clients. Invited to assist, she took the child off the ball and allowed her to walk on her toes and press up against the wall where she quickly became calm. By lifting the girl off the ground and asking her to balance, the physical therapist had removed the few means the child had to orient herself to the world and had forced her into intimate contact with a giant who didn't speak her language and for all purposes was dragging her off to another planet. This was a dramatic, if not traumatic, example of the difference between meeting a child where he or she is at and working from there, and imposing the therapist's will. Collaboration between the two staff members inevitably improved the quality of care for this child.

The techniques of dance/movement therapy are almost as limitless as movement itself, making it an adaptable modality to children of all ages. A young blind child may benefit from a combination of structured and improvisational exercises set to music, gradually expanding his/her repertoire of movement, expression of feeling, and ways of communicating and navigating in the world. A school age hyperactive child might be introduced to a sequence of movement "games," each one directed at slightly more sophisticated body control and learning of relaxation skills. An anorexic might benefit from changes in body image and a growing respect for the needs and pleasures to be derived from one's own body. A withdrawn schizophrenic boy might participate with others in a group dance for the first time in years, trusting people enough to hold hands, and experience the tangible closeness and distance of others as he moves in a circle of equally vulnerable partners. For many children, this form of therapy offers a much needed opportunity to integrate and celebrate as whole the various parts of themselves.

9

The On-Site Therapeutic Technique

TYPES OF PROBLEMS

Independence Training; Infant Stimulation; Phobias; Travel Training; Work Adjustment.

Indicators

The on-site technique of psychotherapy occurs at the physical place where the child or adolescent is having difficulty and therefore is most appropriate for clients who cannot generalize what they learn in therapy outside the office.

Contraindicators

Since the on-site technique requires a commitment of concentrated blocks of time by the therapist, it is generally done in a short amount of time, usually not over a month. Problems that might require treatment over an extended period of time might be better handled in milieu therapy. For example, an infant who needed more than a month's worth of concentrated home visits by a therapist might benefit more from the treatment available in specialized therapeutic daycare centers. Since the on-site technique is a very intrusive approach, it may be contraindicated for clients who would be embarrassed or inhibited by being in public with a professional.

THERAPEUTIC PRINCIPLES

On-site therapy*, where the treatment is done in the client's home, community, workplace, or school, can be effective when everything else has failed. It can help keep handicapped clients from being institutionalized or from losing their jobs. It can help parents more effectively meet the needs of their atypical infants, preventing the development of much more serious problems. It seems to be the treatment of choice for nearly all severely phobic children. It may have even wider applications as it becomes more accepted as an alternative to traditional approaches.

Of course, practicing psychotherapy outside the office is really not new at all. Even Freud was known to have his patients over as houseguests, and he took at least one on vacation with him so that his

---

*On-site therapy is also referred to as "contextual therapy," a phrase coined by Dr. Manuel Zane in his work with phobics.

analysis could continue uninterrupted. Many therapists make school visits to observe children and any therapist working in an institution or hospital setting will be constantly using his/her skills in the child's living environment. However, what is new about the on-site technique of psychotherapy is the systematic treatment of the child exclusively in the place and at the time where the problems most frequently exist.

Although on-site therapeutic techniques can be extremely effective—sometimes the only effective treatment for specific disorders—there are certainly good reasons why therapists may be reluctant to venture out of their offices into the cold, unpredictable world. There are practical problems like time management and cost figuring; ethical problems revolving around the artificiality of having a therapist in the day-to-day life of a client; and, when a therapist steps out of his or her office, many of the traditional rules and techniques of therapy are changed. For example, what would you do as a therapist in the following situations?

> "You are working with a mildly handicapped child who is having extreme behavioral problems both at home and in his school. As you enter the house on your third on-site session, the child's mother indicates that she would like to talk to you more about how she sees the problem when you are done working with the child."
>
> "You are working with a child who is phobic toward escalators. While doing treatment in a department store, you are addressed by a friend of the family who has recognized the child and is wondering what you are doing with her."
>
> "When you arrive for an appointment at a child's home, he is throwing a tantrum in his bedroom and refused to come out."
>
> "You are working with a mother to help her learn how to stimulate her blind infant. The treatment is proceeding very smoothly when one day the mother brings up her suspicions that her husband is having an affair and wants your advice on what to do."

Practical Issues

On-site therapy is usually performed in concentrated blocks of time, sometimes as much as 4 or 5 hours a day, 5 days a week. When properly used, the on-site therapy technique is definitely cost-effective for the client. Therapy is usually accomplished in a fraction of the time that it would take to address the same problem through conventional therapy, and usually at significantly less cost. But scheduling on-site treatments can be a constant juggling act for a busy therapist. The therapy must take place at the time and place that the client's problems occur, rather than at the therapist's convenience. Since the treatment is both rapid and intense, it would be virtually impossible for a therapist to have more than one on-site client and still maintain an office practice. This problem can be overcome, however, by the use of therapy assistants.

While I have usually worked with masters-level psychologists as therapy assistants, graduate students and even trained volunteers can be used to implement many types of programs. Obviously the degree of skill and training required of the therapeutic assistant will vary according to the type of problem being treated. The primary advantage of using therapy assistants is that they have a more flexible schedule and can accommodate themselves to be with the client at the times when they are most needed. They also usually work at a lower hourly rate than the primary therapist, reducing the cost of therapy for the client's family. Even when therapy assistants are used, however, it is still the responsibility of the primary therapist to know the child, his environment, and his problems, as if the primary therapist were actually providing the treatment. This means doing the assessment, writing the treatment plan, observing the therapy as it progresses, and closely supervising the therapy assistant.

The other major practical problem using this technique of psychotherapy is dealing with the geographic distance of the clients from the therapist's office. While this problem may sometimes be cumbersome, it is not insurmountable. In most cases I feel that if clients live close enough to be referred to me, then they are close enough for the primary or assistant therapist to go to them. In many cases the location of the client will be a factor in selecting an assistant. I was once able to treat a client who lived forty miles from my office by using an assistant who lived in that same community and who only had to travel to see me once a week for supervision. Typically, the on-site technique is carried out in 2- to 3-hour blocks of time and sometimes more, to avoid the need for unnecessary travelling. There are many other practical issues that have to be considered as a therapist begins to provide on-site treatment programs. If assistants are hired, they will have to be supervised closely. Since they will be working for you, under your license, you will have to consider whether or not they are covered under your liability insurance, how they will be paid, and how you can best monitor their work without making them feel that you are restricting their own therapeutic knowledge and creativity.

While these and other practical problems must be taken into account, I view them as minor hurdles in this type of treatment, a treatment that can have a profound effect on a client's life. Thorough planning before the treatment begins is always the best insurance against unwelcome surprises.

Ethical Considerations

Stepping into a patient's daily life in order to provide the best method of treatment for him/her takes daring and courage on the part of the therapist. It is outside the normal realm of our training and experience and puts our theories right on the line. But it is also an artificial intrusion on our clients and their families and should not be undertaken lightly. For this reason, therapy should not proceed without a written contract outlining just what can be expected from the therapy and what cannot. In many cases I will "guarantee" that I will be able to achieve the objectives that have been designated in the therapy plan; if they are not met, I will rewrite the objectives and continue to work with the client and/or his family without a fee until the new objectives are realized. The contract generally looks like other therapy plans as described in Chapter 2, but in addition I include a detailed, hourly cost analysis of the therapy. This breakdown will include not only the hourly charges for the therapy, but any additional charges such as travel time, the costs of unusual materials, charges for reports, and so forth. As in other therapy plans, the results that can be expected from the therapy are stated as behavioral objectives that clearly detail how the criterion for success is to be measured.

A related ethical concern in on-site therapy is the issue of confidentiality. As in all forms of psychotherapy, clients have a right to privacy regarding their treatment, and the therapist has the responsibility to protect that right in all circumstances. But what happens if relatives drop in while the therapist is in the home, or a neighbor inquires about "that woman" seen accompanying the child to and from school? The privacy of the therapy is suddenly public. Each circumstance will be handled differently, but it is the therapist's job at the onset of therapy to make sure that the family understands the issue of confidentiality and has anticipated the situations that might come up. Excessive concern about what others may think may indicate to the therapist that this therapeutic technique is contraindicated.

Another more subtle ethical consideration has to do with the role of the therapist in working with a family in the home or community. All our cultural mores will push the therapist and his or her clients to personalize the therapeutic relationship. There are no social rules for having a therapist come into a client's home; each may, quite naturally, turn to the common rules of social etiquette. But the therapist must never lose sight of his or her role as a professional. When I am using on-site techniques, I follow the same formal social etiquette that I use in the office. As one experienced therapist put it, when it comes to social etiquette the therapist should treat the client as a formal guest. I believe that the same rule holds true for therapy done outside the confines of the office. A therapist who is overly solicitous and responds to the client as to a neighbor or a friend, loses objectivity; with the loss of objectivity goes the therapist's professional standing. Stepping out of the formal role as therapist, even just a little bit, implies promises to the client and/or his family that the therapist can't keep.

Issues of Technique

Another reason that the therapist must remain formal and objective when working on-site is to anticipate and therapeutically deal with the family dynamics. Each individual person should be considered as part of a larger family system, as if he/she were in the office.

Complex and powerful dynamics are always operating. Some members will try to get the therapist to ally with them, some will reject help, and others will become dependent on the therapist and think that he/she can do no wrong. The therapist's specific approach to the family will vary according to his/her particular orientation, as well as on the stated objectives of the therapy plan. On entering into the lives of any family, the therapist will see many conflicts and problems. While it is the therapist's ethical responsibility to identify these problems and suggest potential remedies, the therapist should not directly intervene unless it has been designated in the therapy contract that he or she should do so. Of course, if the problem of another family member is impeding the progress of the client, then the therapist must meet with the family and rewrite the contract to reflect this new knowledge. An extreme example of this type of situation might involve an alcoholic father who verbally abused other family members including the phobic child the therapist was hired to work with. In this situation, continuing to treat the child without first restructuring the family dynamics would be fruitless.

On the other end of the continuum are family members who seek out the therapist for their problems and concerns that are not related to the problem of the client. Again, while these problems may be real, it would be no more appropriate to treat the problems in the context of doing on-site therapy then it would be to treat problems brought to the attention of the therapist at a dinner party. If approached by a family member (or anyone else in the client's life), the therapist should try to clarify his or her role in implementing the treatment plan for the identified client. The therapist should then invite the family member to schedule an appointment at some convenient time.

On a day to day basis, the ethical problems, practical concerns, and questions of therapy technique tend to blend together, and although there are many guidelines, each therapist will have to develop his or her own "style" in handling these issues. Let's return to the hypothetical scenarios that I presented at the beginning of this chapter. I have noted my reactions based on my experience in similar circumstances and derived from my training in analytically oriented therapy and a systems approach to families. Your reactions may be different; however they should be consonant with your theories, your experience of doing psychotherapy, and the specific techniques that you have chosen to use "on-site" with your client.

    1. *Problem:* You are working with a mildly handicapped child who is having extreme behavioral problems both at home and in his school. As you enter the house on your third on-site session, the child's mother indicates that she would like to talk to you more about how she sees the problem when you are done working with the child. *Response:* I would explain to her that although I'm sure what she has to say is important, I plan each session out carefully and need to leave exactly when it is over. I would invite her to schedule an appointment with me at the office by calling me later that day. If I think that this is an attempt of the mother to try and develop a special relationship with me as a way of acting out some dynamic of the family system, then I would explain when she called that I would prefer to discuss these issues with all the family members present, and I would ask if she and the rest of the family could come in for an appointment.

    2. *Problem:* You are working with a child who is phobic toward escalators. While doing treatment in a department store, you are addressed by a friend of the family who has recognized the child and is wondering what you are doing with her. *Response:* If possible, I would avoid identifying myself as a therapist out of respect for the family's right to confidentiality. If the friend was worried about the child being out with a stranger, I would reassure him/her as needed. Fortunately, this is rarely a problem. Anyone who might know the child and might also see you with him or her in public would also see that you had a special caring relationship and that there was no need to worry. If you work in a community where this is likely to happen often, then this possibility should be discussed thoroughly with the family beforehand, and you should help each family member come to terms with his/her own feelings. Typically, you will be working in on-site situations where the client's problems will have already become public to some degree, and each family member may have feelings of guilt, shame, and anger.

    3. *Problem:* When you arrive for an appointment at a child's home, he is throwing a tantrum in his bedroom and refuses to come out. *Response:* This can be an extremely awkward situation, with each person thinking, "Just who is the authority here?" The parents might feel that since it is their home, they must handle the situation. But then again, they see the therapist as the identified "expert," so they may want to see just what you do. You can ease this situation by being very clear about what *you* think is appropriate for the stated therapeutic goals.

Let's say, for example, that one of the therapeutic goals is to help the parents learn to handle their child's tantrums. In this case you are fortunate to have an example of the behavior to work with (although you probably won't feel quite so lucky at the time). Then, whether you model how to handle the child or whether you want one or both parents to intervene will depend on where you are in the treatment program. If, on the other hand, this is unusual behavior for the child, it may be an expression of his anxiety at having you in his home or a more general conflict having to do with the nature of treating his particular problem. In this case you must bring the same intuitive empathy and therapeutic skills that you would have with any child who is hurting, and with patience and understanding the therapeutic bond between you and the child will be strengthened.

4. *Problem:* You are working with a mother to help her learn how to stimulate her blind infant. The treatment is proceeding very smoothly when one day the mother brings up her suspicions that her husband is having an affair and wants your advice on what to do. *Response:* As in example number one, I would stick to the therapy plan for that session, taking note of the mother's concern and anxiety only so far as it relates to the care of her infant. The therapist's role in on-site therapy is not one of counselor or confidante. He or she should stick to the therapeutic task at hand and handle other problems in their own time and place.

Phobias: A Five Year Old
Who Wouldn't Go to School

If I hadn't been standing at her doorstep when the large yellow bus wheeled to a stop in front of her house, I might have thought, like the school psychologist who diagnosed her, that Tina had a school phobia. But she wasn't afraid of going to school. She was afraid of the school's bus. I watched as she turned pale at the sight of the bus, frozen in terror until it pulled away. This, her mother had explained, had happened every day for two weeks since the beginning of kindergarten. That day, I rode with Tina and her mother in the car to the elementary school about two miles away, and I was struck by how calm and relaxed she looked making up songs in the back seat. But as we pulled into the school parking lot, Tina stiffened again, holding her stomach and complaining that she felt she was going to be sick. I noticed that she wasn't looking at the school, as I would have anticipated—she was staring at the parking lot full of school buses.

Tina entered her classroom stiffly, like a robot. Since she was having such a hard time adjusting to school, her teacher suggested that she only stay for an hour each morning until she was more used to it, and directed her mother to the teacher's lounge. As her mother turned to go, I was again surprised at Tina's reaction. She hardly seemed to notice her mother's leaving. She went into the block corner, said "Hello" to another little girl, and started to play.

The assessment is just one area of treating a phobic child where the therapist who is working on-site is at an advantage. The irrational nature of phobias, in adults as well as in children, often belies understanding, and treating the patient away from the actual phobic experience obscures the problem more. In Tina's case no one had ever noticed that she was afraid of buses. She always rode in the family car and as far as could be recalled had never been on a bus before. Nor could anyone remember any particular event that might have led to such a fear. Tina was always timid and withdrawn, an only child who was kept at home rather than sent to nursery school because her mother reported: "She just doesn't seem to like other kids that much." She had had nightmares since the age of two, but these seemed to have diminished in their frequency and intensity in the six months before she began school.

The entire treatment for Tina's fear of buses lasted two weeks, at which time she was riding in the school bus to and from school and remaining there for the full four hours of the kindergarten program. The parents were seen for biweekly sessions for three months more so that they could learn ways to foster their daughter's newly found independence. A six month follow-up showed that Tina had made an excellent adjustment to school and was considered to be one of the more outgoing children in the class.

A more traditional, office-bound approach to Tina's problem would have taken up to three times as long—much too long a time considering that this was a critical developmental point for Tina, one where she could have easily regressed or become fixated.

To understand why on-site therapy is so much more expedient and precise than an office approach in working with phobic children, it might be worthwhile to do a comparison between the therapy done with Tina, and the therapy I might have used in the office.

On-Site Therapy

Assessment:

The assessment of the phobia took three hours one morning with the client and her mother in observation and interview.

Treatment:

The treatment began the next day, a technique of systematic desensitization toward buses, done in nine two-hour sessions.

Session 1

Tina was taught how to relax and breathe deeply when she was upset. She practiced this technique while looking at pictures of buses, and standing on her front porch pretending the school bus was coming. Tina spent an hour in her class afterwards.

Session 2

We talked about buses and why they were scary to Tina. We read a story about school buses and practiced progressive relaxation. Tina spent an hour and ten minutes in her class afterwards.

Session 3

We walked around the neighborhood looking for buses and counting them. We went back to the house and drew pictures of the buses we saw. Tina spent an hour and a half in her class later that morning.

Session 4

Tina and I waited for the school bus to arrive in the morning, and then as we had prearranged, walked half-way to the bus door, waved to the driver, and watched the bus pull away. All this time Tina practiced her deep breathing

Office Therapy

Assessment:

The assessment would take two to five hours, probably scheduled in two or more separate visits. It would consist of an interview with the mother, a fear rating scale, one or more projective tests, and observation of the child's play. All the information about the fear would be inferred.

Treatment

Sessions 1–4

The initial session would be devoted to finding out more about the exact nature of the fear, and would include the exposure of various stimuli to the child in the form of pictures, sounds, toys, videotaped sequences, and so forth. The child's reaction to each stimulus would be recorded and rated according to the degree of anxiety that was manifested. The stimuli would then be organized into a hierarchy from the least to the most anxiety provoking stimuli. With fifty minute sessions, twice a week, this would take about two weeks.

Sessions 5–27

The principles of symstematic and progressive relation would also be used in the office, beginning with the stimulus that was least anxiety provoking in the hierarchy. As each stimulus, or set of stimuli was presented, the child would be instructed to relax until a minimum of anxiety was present. This procedure, continuing on through the hierarchy, could take two months, meeting twice a week. In addition, the parents would have to be trained to use the same technique with their child at home; this might take another four sessions. (This would not, however, be the same as a family therapy that would work on the causes of the and muscle relaxation. We then drove to school and Tina had a friendly talk with the school bus driver ten feet away from the bus.

Session 5

A repeat of session 4, but when the bus arrived, we walked up to the open door to say hello to the driver; later when we met the driver at school, she asked Tina if she would like to see the inside of the bus. We all went in and the bus driver told us funny anecdotes about driving a bus. We stayed in the bus for 15 minutes. Tina went to her class for the remaining 2 hours, staying through lunch.

Session 6

Tina and I greeted the bus in the morning, went in and sat near the driver. We rode for one block and then got out and walked the rest of the way to school. It was pretty tiring. We repeated the same procedure when her class was over at 1:00 p.m.

Session 7

Same as session 6, but we rode for four blocks on the bus to and from school.

Session 8

We rode the entire way to and from school. I sat next to Tina on the way over, but about half-way through I changed seats with one of her friends in the class. On the way back Tina sat next to her friend, and I sat near the driver.

Session 9

Tina rode to and from school by herself. I saw her off and was there when she returned after school to say goodbye. We had ice cream and cake to celebrate Tina's graduation.

problem. If indicated, family therapy would take four to ten more sessions.)

Comparing these two types of therapy, done by the same therapist, for the same problem, we can see that the office therapy would take twenty-seven or more therapy hours over two to three months, while the on-site therapy would be accomplished in twenty-two hours of work with the child, in nine sessions over a period of two weeks. Even if the two techniques were equally effective, the on-site technique would have the child in school and past an important developmental hurdle in less than one-tenth the time.

Work Adjustment Training

I have seen many job training programs for the mild to moderately intellectually handicapped, programs that train clients for work in electronic assembly, messenger services, janitorial work, kitchen work, beautician services, clerical work, and so forth. But even the best of these programs can't anticipate the kinds of problems that might come up on an actual job.

Carl B. had been in a special education school since the age of five; at the age of 15 he had been enrolled in a prevocational training program emphasizing kitchen skills. He could do salad preparation, bussing, general clean-up, and dishwashing, but what he most enjoyed was making sandwiches for the school lunch programs. When he graduated from school and found a job, however, it was in a small diner. They didn't need salad preparation, because their salads were bought ready-made. They used paper plates at a single counter so there was no dishwashing or tables to clean up. What they primarily needed Carl to do was to slice the meats for their submarine sandwiches and to do the janitorial work. Neither of these were problems for Carl. They also needed him to go through a twice daily checklist to see what kinds of supplies needed to be ordered, what frozen meats needed to be defrosted, and what ingredients needed to be put out for the pizza chef. The mechanics of these tasks were easy enough for Carl, but his academic skills were only at a second grade level, and he couldn't read the checklist.

Having known Carl for some time, I offered to supervise an on-site training program to prepare him for the job. I promised his employer that within a week Carl would be able to do every aspect of the job as well as, if not better than, the previous employee. A few days later I reported for work with Carl and listened while the manager explained Carl's various duties. Except for the supplies checklist, Carl was familiar with all of the other job requirements and seemed to catch on immediately to the routine. The diner had a very informal atmosphere, but since Carl was used to working on a strict schedule in his vocational training program, I made up a time schedule for him as he performed each of his required job functions. Since he could tell time only to the half hour, we used the half hour as the basic time unit and made up a time chart for his duties in picture form.

It was clear that the manager of the diner and the other employees had never seen anything quite like us—Carl, with his spotless overalls, and I with a clipboard and stopwatch, looking like an efficiency expert for a large corporation. But no one seemed to mind, and when Carl did all the work in one morning that had taken the last employee all day to accomplish, the manager was delighted. He immediately thought of several more maintenance jobs that he had put off for years that Carl could begin on in the afternoon.

That left only the supplies checklist to be tackled. The manager showed us around the storeroom and the walk-in refrigerator and pointed out all the supplies that had to be monitored daily. I drew a schematic drawing of the room, indicating what the manager had explained were the maximum and minimum of each type of stock that he wanted to have on hand. There were twenty-five items in all. The manager then took us over to where the pizza chef was cooking, and showed us how his ingredients were laid out on the counter. Each ingredient had its own container that Carl had to refill twice a day from the supply room.

That evening, I redrew the illustration I had made of the supply room, indicating the subtraction that Carl would have to do in order to determine what had to be reordered. The next day I met Carl after lunch at the diner to train him to use his checklist. Although Carl couldn't read, I thought that he could match the words from the schematic checklist with a label on each product, but that proved to be too slow and cumbersome. So, to aid in matching the products to the checklist, we numbered each of the items and put a corresponding two-inch high plastic stick-on number on the location of each of the supplies in the storeroom. We practiced finding each of the products in the storeroom and matching it to the corresponding place on the checklist. Carl then practiced counting each item and entered each count on the appropriate box in the checklist. When the twenty-five items were checked, Carl then sat down with a calculator to determine how much of each item needed to be reordered. Although he could do simple subtraction, Carl often made mistakes and said that math "gave him a headache." Using a calculator, however, appealed to Carl's newfound sophistication.

It took just under two and a half hours to teach Carl how to use the supplies checklist and another half hour to teach him how to use the calculator and to transfer the numbers on the checklist to a standard reordering form for the manager. While it took Carl longer to check the supplies than it might take with someone without a handicap, Carl more than made up for this loss of time in his diligence in other tasks. After a few weeks when Carl was thoroughly familiar with the stockroom, we were able to do away with the schematic drawing and the calculator and use a checklist that Carl could handwrite for the manager. Carl had made a step into community employment that might not have been possible without the aid of on-site training. The total treatment time: 6 hours, in one and a half days.

10
Hypnotherapy

TYPE OF PROBLEM

Anxiety; Eating Disorders; Pain Control; Phobias; Psychogenic Problems (asthma, cyclic vomiting); Sleep Disturbances.

Indicators

Hypnotherapy can be used with children ages three and up, but it is particularly appropriate for children in the age range of seven to fourteen. Children who are creative and can sustain rich mental images are the best hypnotic candidates, but techniques can also be effective for children and adolescents who are very concrete in their thinking.

Contraindicators

I usually do not attempt hypnotherapy with latency age children and adolescents who are extremely resistant or defiant. Children who are very active and can hardly sit still *may* be treated with hypnotic techniques, as may children who have significant deficits in their mental abilities; however, this would not be my choice of treatment for these clients. A strong intractable prejudice against hypnosis, usually by the parents, would be a contraindication, as would a belief that hypnosis is some sort of magic or exorcism.

THERAPEUTIC PRINCIPLES

Hypnosis, and by association hypnotherapy, have gotten a lot of bad press. People often associate hypnosis with magic shows, stage performances, mind control, and various kinds of unethical behavior. There are many myths about hypnosis and hypnotherapy, myths that need to be dispelled, both to the reader and to prospective patients for whom these techniques might be appropriate.

First of all, hypnosis does not imply loss of control by the subjects, whether they are children or adults. The patients do not go to sleep, nor do they forget who they are, where they are, or what they are doing. In fact the vast majority of patients who are helped by hypnosis report they are completely aware of everything that is happening. Only a relatively small percentage, estimated at less than five or ten percent of the population, experience the type of trance state that is popularized by TV and drama, where the subject appears to be asleep and is unaware of his immediate environment. The hypnotic state is a relatively normal and common experience in both children and adults. Daydreaming, being lost in a TV show or a story, and doing certain kinds of mechanical repetitive tasks so that you are hardly conscious of what you are doing are all examples of trancelike states. They are only different from what we call hypnosis in that there are no suggestions being made to the person from a therapist, and the subject is not consciously cooperating in a process aimed at helping them.

Adults, and to a lesser extent adolescents and children, may come in with specific fears about hypnosis. They might be afraid to undergo hypnosis because they might not "come out" of it. This is a myth because the subject remains in control of himself or herself throughout the entire period of hypnosis. Another patient might feel that he or she could be made to do unethical or inappropriate things that would later be regretted. This is highly unlikely, if not impossible. The vast majority of clients state that they are aware through the entire process that they are being hypnotized and do not feel they are being manipulated.

When parents are worried about their children, the parents may need to be reminded and reassured that the therapist is working only in the interest of the client. In some cases the parent may be so anxious that he/she should be invited to observe behind a two-way mirror or to watch a videotape of the therapist working with another client in order to demystify this type of treatment. If the right equipment is not available, and there are no specific contraindications, the parent may be invited to remain in the room with the child and can even take part in the hypnotic experience if he/she wishes.

Since each person has his own individual misconceptions, the therapist needs to take the time to ask both the child and the parents what they know and think about hypnosis and to allay any fears and dispel any myths that exist. Strong fears and anxieties may be a contraindication for using the technique.

There is a long-standing debate on what hypnotherapy is. Most researchers and clinicians agree that hypnotherapy is an altered state of consciousness whereby the patient uses his or her abilities to concentrate and block stimulation that would otherwise be present in the environment. In theory, this hyperconcentration makes the subject amenable to suggestions and motivated to change. The greatest difference of opinion comes in describing whether this state of concentration is actually any different from any other type of concentration. The argument boils down to whether or not there exists such a thing as a "trance" or whether the subject is simply experiencing something new and experiences a "trance" to please the therapist.

In clinical practice the trance-versus-nontrance debate is not significant. Whatever kind of psychological phenomenon hypnosis represents, it is a technique that draws on universal human experiences and appears to have wide applications.

Hypnotherapy can be divided into three phases—the induction, the process whereby the patient goes into an altered state or a trance state; the treatment itself, when a specific set of suggestions are made to the patient; and a post-hypnotic state, where the actual change in the patient's emotions, thoughts, and behavior must occur.

The induction can be done in many different ways, both with children and adults. To be hypnotized, the patient must be in a relaxed, highly concentrated state and at least marginally receptive toward the suggestion of change. For very young children the induction may take the form of some simple repetitive task such as putting blocks in holes and taking them out.

In more formal inductions the child is told to sit and relax and then is given the suggestion to form mental images as if he were watching a movie or TV. The therapist may suggest that the child close his eyes, but this is not necessary. The therapist then may describe a scene, emphasizing concrete visual aspects of the image and ideas that are multisensory to provoke images of sound, taste, sight, and touch. As the child enters a trance state, the therapist points out the natural occurring physiological responses to the client *just as they begin*. The therapist notes: "Your eyelids are heavy and you want to rest" (as he or she observes the eyes beginning to blink and close). "You are breathing slowly and more deeply" (as this is observed). "Your arms are heavy, as if there are weights attached to them" (as it is observed that the child's hands are limp and resting heavily on his/her legs).

As the therapist mentions physiological responses *that have actually already begun to occur*, the child develops a sense of trust that other suggestions, therapeutic suggestions, will also occur.

The therapist, once he or she has observed that the child is focusing inwardly and responding less to outside stimuli, may wish to test the child's suggestibility; however, this is not necessary. Suggestibility scales exist for children as for adults. These scales typically test to see whether the patient will follow specific suggestions such as levitation of hand and arm, immobilization of limbs, inability to open the eyes, and so forth, suggesting that the patient's unconscious mind can act without acknowledgment or even cooperation with the patient's conscious mind. While these scales are considered to be reliable and valid in measuring hypnotizability, there has been no research that correlates the degree of suggestibility with the success of hypnotherapy treatment. In other words, even though a subject may be highly suggestible and go into a trancelike state very easily, this doesn't necessarily mean that this technique will be successful in helping him solve his problem. Conversely, *even though a child or an adult may not appear to be in a highly suggestible state, and he may report feeling absolutely normal, the suggestion that is given may still have a significant therapeutic effect.*

One of the simplest techniques of induction is to have patients open their eyes on the count of one, close their eyes on the count of two, open them on the count of three, close them on the count of four, and so forth, up to a hundred. The therapist comments: "At any time you may feel the need to keep your eyes closed and to let them remain closed." This suggestion has several components. First, it relies on the therapist's knowledge of the physiological certainty that the patient's eyes will tire of opening and closing before the therapist counts to 100. The therapist may speed up the count to speed up the patient's weariness. He/she may skip numbers in a random order, thus confusing the patient and only allowing the patient to escape the confusion by accepting the suggestion that the patient's eyes "may soon wish to close." The therapist should offer suggestions in the context of a choice that the patient can make ("Your eyes will close whenever you like.") The physiological and psychological dice are loaded so that the eyes almost certainly will close; if they do not, neither the patient nor the therapist has failed, because the patient has simply chosen that they will not close and the therapist only presented the choice—he did not *dictate* that the eyes will close. In the event that the eyes close, the therapist may then wish to continue testing the patient's suggestibility by seeing if he/she will receive a suggestion that the eyes will not open. The therapist comments: "Your eyelids feel as if they are *stuck* together. As if they are *glued shut . . . heavy* as lead . . . Even though *you may wish* to open them, they will probably *stay closed*. The eyes want to stay closed . . . stay closed . . . closed." (Italicized words are emphasized.)

Because of the voice inflections, use of repetition, and emphasis on what the therapist is aiming toward, a division is made between the patient's conscious and unconscious motivation. In this instance, the patient knows that he can open his eyes, but he wants to keep them shut to please the therapist (as some theories suggest) or perhaps because of the force of the suggestions themselves. If the patient does not take the suggestion and, in fact, chooses to prove that he can consciously control his eyes, this again is not taken as a failure, but rather a choice. The therapist may simply respond that "your eyes are not yet ready to stay shut but you may want to close them sometime later." By accepting all behaviors in this manner, the therapist does not fight the patient, but rather always remains on the side of the patient's desire to control his behavior and to use this control for therapeutic change.

As an experienced hypnotherapist will tell you, the method of induction is relatively unimportant compared with the second stage of hypnotherapy where the treatment occurs. In this stage the child or adolescent receives suggestions that will help him cope with his problem in a new way. The treatment itself will vary according to the particular problem, the abilities and age of the child, and according to the interests and other idiosyncrasies that make each child an individual. Although a skilled therapist may have preset ideas as to the specific type of suggestions that will be useful, he/she must also keep an open mind and a skilled eye to determine how the child is reacting and what effect the suggestions are having. The following are some examples of the types of suggestions that can work with children.

Pain Control

There are many different types of suggestions for the control of pain, since this is one of the areas in which hypnosis is used most widely. Inductions may be used with transient pain as well as with intractible pain, so I will give examples of both.

A hypnotherapist working at a sickle cell anemia clinic recently told me of a young child who came in experiencing extreme panic at the thought of giving blood. As in many types of anticipated pain, or other medical procedures that children are afraid of, it is difficult to separate children's anxiety and panic from their actual physical experiences. In this case the therapist, after a quick induction, had the eight-year-old imagine that she was out in the snow building a snowman. As the child relaxed, she was given very concrete suggestions that she could feel exactly as if she were in the snow and could feel the coldness and the wetness and the wind and the taste of snow. She was delighted with the image as she saw herself tumbling and sledding down a snow-covered hill near her house. The therapist then suggested that she take a snowball and put it on her arm just where the needle was going to go. It was very cold—so cold, in fact, that it numbed the arm entirely. The arm could feel nothing but the cold. It could not possibly feel the pain. The therapist demonstrated this was true by pinching the child's arm where the needle would go, and, in fact, the child had no experience of pain whatsoever. Minutes later the child who had been hysterical at the thought of giving blood confidently waved to the lab technician and held out her arm, much to the surprise of her parents and doctor.

In another case a hypnotherapist on an oncology ward was treating a child with cancer, who had periods of very severe pain. The therapist explained to the child that the brain could control all sensations in the body and was, in fact, like a little computer sending out signals to various limbs and muscles and organs. Each path that carried a message to the computer was described as a cable; each cable was a different color and led to a colored light in the brain. At the site of the pain, particularly in the arms and feet, were switches; when the nerves were on, the switches were open and the lights were on. When the nerves were off, the switches were closed and the lights were off. While the therapist was with the child, he suggested that the child experience some of the pain; the child was able to do this. The therapist then told the child to turn off that switch where the pain was. To slowly turn if off and the light would grow dimmer and dimmer until, in fact, it was completely off and the place that once hurt now had no pain and felt perfectly comfortable and perfectly natural. And so the child learned, through concrete images, to concentrate on turning off the pain—controlling the pain so that it was hardly experienced—no more than a very dull ache—and sometimes it was not experienced at all. Other people, including the child's nurses and parents, were also taught to use this hypnotic procedure and to encourage the child with these suggestions to control his pain.

Psychogenic Disorders

Olness and Gardner (1978) note that "hypnotherapy has been found to be effective as an ancillary therapy in treating numerous problems connected with the autonomic nervous system including: asthma, nausea, vomiting, hypertension, hyperhydrosis, recurrent hives, bleeding, urine retention, globus hystericus, and hiccoughs." They state that although these problems will often be treated by other means, hypnotherapy can be used to relieve symptoms. However, they also caution that the secondary gains for these symptoms are important considerations and that the child who may learn to stop wheezing in a hospital room surrounded by friendly staff, may not be willing to do so when he/she is at home craving attention. The treatment techniques for these psychophysiological disorders will generally use the components of relaxation and imagery that were discussed in the treatment of pain, helping the child to use concrete images to dilate the vascular system, relax specific muscle groups, and so forth. Often the support and suggestions of the hypnosis itself can be enough to convince the child that he can control some of the symptoms. For example a 9-year-old eneuretic learned that she could control her symptoms in two sessions by paying attention to her body signals and by imaging control of her bladder while she slept.

Habit Control

In working with habit disorders, which might include nail biting, thumb sucking, hair pulling, tics, insomnia, and eating problems, I generally combine hypnotherapy with the techniques developed by Asner and

Young's *Habit Control In a Day* (1977). These authors emphasize the following method: 1. accurate records of habit episodes are kept, 2. the social effects of the habits are considered, 3. the patient is directed toward paying attention to the mannerisms and behaviors that precede the habit episode, 4. the patient is taught to identify situations, activities, and people that cause the habit to occur, and finally 5. the patient is encouraged to practice and rehearse a competing habit which will interfere with the problem and yet be socially acceptable. Hypnosis is particularly helpful in steps 3, 4, and 5.

   For example, in the treatment of a ten-year-old girl who sucked her thumb both at school and at home, I began by having her put a check in a notebook each time she was aware that she was sucking her thumb. This data-keeping reduced the habit behavior simply by drawing her attention to it and making the child conscious of what she was doing. To raise the awareness of the habit, I put her into a light trance in which she was directed to imagine herself in a situation where she was a perfectly comfortable sucking her thumb. She was then told to imagine it would be even more comfortable with her hands relaxed on the desk (the substituting behavior). "Your poor thumb," I told her, "it really isn't so comfortable being wet and chewed on. The thumb, after all, is a part of the body that likes to be comfortable too! The thumb enjoys having the air circulate around it and feeling free to do what thumbs do—to press on the desktop, to twiddle the other thumb, to tap out a melody, to put in a thumbtack, to *do what thumbs do.*" With these suggestions, the child was made to feel comfortable about disassociating the thumb as a mode of oral gratification. The competing, substitution* behaviors included pressing the thumb against the table and twiddling the thumbs. The competing behavior was then practiced under hypnosis and in real life. The girl was directed to practice keeping her thumb out of her mouth and letting it "be free to be a thumb." In one session she decided to put a little face on her thumb and use it as a finger puppet to give the thumb its own "life," differentiating it from her need for oral gratification (which was addressed using other therapy technique).

   Another therapist might have used an aversive technique similar to one used with smokers, whereby the patient would be told under hypnosis that the thumb would have a noxious taste or a horrible smell and it would be so vile and disgusting that she could not possibly want to put it in her mouth. I avoid using these aversive techniques whenever possible, for although they may work, the implications of having a child

---

*Site or place substitution is another type of substitution sometimes used in hypnosis. Here the symptom is not changed at all, but rather the *place* where the symptom resides is changed. A facial tic, for example, might be moved to the hand or foot where it would be less noticeable and more easily treated.

be disgusted with a part of her own body, even so small a part as a thumb, does not seem therapeutic.

The example of thumb sucking is a good illustration of how hypnotherapy can be used to facilitate behavioral principles. Suggestions given to the unconscious support the work with the patient's conscious motivation in affecting a change.

The third phase of hypnotherapy is the most important one since it is there that the patient changes his/her real life patterns. Sometimes the therapist will make tapes of the sessions for the child or adolescent to use at home, but more often he/she will use post-hypnotic suggestions.

Contrary to popular opinion, post-hypnotic suggestions are usually remembered by the subject and are done with his or her full cooperation. While the client is still under hypnosis, the therapist may suggest that with a given signal the client will experience comfort, relaxation, or some other appropriate affective state that he or she has experienced in hypnosis. The signal may be one under the client's control, such as clasping his/her hands together to feel more confident when going to the dentist. Or it may be an external cue, such as hearing the school bell ring and being motivated to concentrate on schoolwork. Usually the client is trained in the office to respond to this signal. For instance in the example of the school bell, the therapist might ring a bell and have the client go into a state of relaxation and this would be practiced over several days.

Tape recordings of hypnotic sessions which are played back at home are usually only effective when the client is highly motivated to change. If there is no motivation, the child or adolescent may find it convenient to lose the tape or the tape recorder or to forget to practice this technique.

Gardner (1974) suggests that aside from the alleviation of symptoms, hypnotherapy can be useful in ego strengthening techniques, such as guiding the child toward such positive feelings as confidence, trust, and mastery in dealing with certain problems. In helping an older child or adolescent deal with a trauma, hypnotherapists will sometimes use the trance state to have the patient "relive" the experience in his or her imagination with gentle guided support.

To sum up, there has been a new interest in hypnotherapy techniques in the last few years and this seems to slowly be expanding itself toward the treatment of children. The creativity and imagination inherent in this technique makes it a particularly appropriate skill for the child therapist to learn and apply in short-term treatment.

11
Biofeedback

TYPES OF PROBLEMS

Anxiety; Hyperactivity; Pain Reduction; Phobias

Indicators

This technique is recommended for children or adolescents who have little or no control over their body states (for example, they cannot relax). It may be particularly appropriate for chldren who have an interest in science or mechanical gadgets.

Contraindicators

Biofeedback would be contraindicated for children who are wary about using machines. These would include tactically defensive children who would be anxious about being physically connected in any way to a machine. Some children with prepsychotic or psychotic symptoms may have delusions about machines that would also contraindicate the use of biofeedback equipment.

THERAPEUTIC PRINCIPLES

Biofeedback can be defined as any organized way in which a patient is immediately shown the degree of his/her physiological responsiveness. A patient who takes his blood pressure daily because of a fear of heart attacks is utilizing a biofeedback technique. A runner who judges his or her endurance by a pulse rate is using biofeedback. In the laboratory and in the clinic the measurement of a wide variety of physiological changes such as muscle tension, skin temperature, electrical impulses of the skin, metabolic rate, and brain wave patterns are all examples of biofeedback, when these changes are made known immediately and continuously to the patient.

Biofeedback assumes that when a patient has a continual knowledge of his physiological state, he may eventually learn to control this state to his own advantage, producing a physiological state associated with relaxation and health rather than tension and anxiety.

The use of "feeding-back" physiological information to children or adolescents is a relatively new science. The benefits can be significant, however, and research has claimed success in working with such diverse problems as asthma, pulmonary insufficiency, migraines, and the physical rehabilitation of stroke, cerebral palsy, and multiple sclerosis victims.

There are many different types of biofeedback instrumentation. A well equipped laboratory that could treat a variety of complaints would cost thousands of dollars and would be prohibitive for most clinicians to whom this book is addressed. For that reason, I will primarily emphasize cases where I used relatively inexpensive instruments costing under one hundred dollars.* To learn about more elaborate methods, the interested reader should refer to *Stress and the Art of Feedback* by Barbara Brown (1977).

There are currently four major psychophysiological processes that are measured by biofeedback instrumentation although, as I mentioned earlier, any physical process that can be measured, with the information immediately being sent back to the patient, would be deemed as biofeedback.

Electromiograph feedback is considered to have the widest range of application (Brown, 1977). The electromiograph or EMG tests the electrical activity of specific muscles or muscle groups. When muscles are tense, they give out more electrical firings, although people may not be aware of this until the tension actually becomes pain. Small sensors that can detect very minimal amounts of tension are placed on the skin over the muscle. EMG biofeedback may be used to either decrease muscle activity, as in controlling pain, or to increase muscle activity, as in the rehabilitation of muscles from partial paralysis. The relative accuracy of EMG biofeedback will depend on the standard placement of the electrodes on the appropriate muscles.

A second type of biofeedback instrumentation relies on the measure of brain wave patterns; this instrument is called an electroencephlogram or EEG. The EEG measures minute microvoltages of electrical activity in the brain from eight or more electrodes placed on the scalp. The electrical activity is then converted into brain wave frequencies that have four (somewhat arbitrarily defined) components— beta, associated with alert behavior and concentration; theta, associated with passive problem solving and creativity; delta, the predominant brain wave pattern exhibited during sleep; and alpha, associated with the meditative daydreaming sometimes called "relaxed wakefulness."

The primary use of EEG biofeedback has involved using the alpha frequency. The popularity of this method among the lay public as well as in clinical settings has led some scientists to begrudge the emergence of an "alpha cult." Scientists are concerned that many people are misled into believing that the alpha state (or any of the other EEG states) is a true psychoneurological process, when in fact each "state" is

---

*It should be noted that this inexpensive equipment does not compare to the equipment found in a biofeedback laboratory in terms of quantitative measurement; however, it is useful in detecting qualitative changes.

an over-simplified brain wave *component* that has questionable validity
or reliability as a measurement tool. Still there are numerous clinical
reports that credit alpha training in reducing pain, epileptic seizures,
and a variety of psychoneurotic disorders.

The third major type of biofeedback instrumentation measures
that peripheral blood flow that changes the temperature on the surface of
the skin. The dilation or restriction of peripheral vessels can change skin
surface temperature so that they fluctuate between 60° and 95° in a
constant room temperature. Minute changes in skin temperature are
measured by a thermistor usually placed on the fingers. Temperature
biofeedback, sometimes abbreviated as TEMP, is typically used for general relaxation and stress related disorders in which internal organs are
predominantly involved.

The last major type of biofeedback instrumentation is the gal-
vonic skin response (GSR) that primarily measures changes in the sym-
pathetic nervous system by recording the chemical change in the sweat
response on the surface of the skin—usually the hand or fingers. When
the patient is more tense or aroused, there are concomitant changes in
the sweat response. GSR biofeedback has been used in the treatment of
anxiety disorders, asthma, and stuttering.

Whatever physiologic process the instrument is measuring,
feedback will take place by either visual or auditory mode, sometimes
both at once. Visually, the subject may be told to watch a needle that
registers a higher number when there is more tension, a printout that
would register an upward slope when there is more tension, or a digital
readout where higher numbers indicate more tension. Auditory feedback is usually in the form of a pure tone that becomes louder and
develops a higher pitch when tension is present and becomes softer and
lower pitched when tension decreases.

The most basic use of biofeedback with children and adolescents
is to teach them relaxation. It should not be surprising that many very
active children with high metabolisms do not know what we mean when
we ask them to calm down, to relax, to concentrate, or to pay attention.
These behaviors are simply not in their repertoire. When we ask a child
to sit down and read, he understands the request or command to stay
seated and he may even be able to control himself to begin the reading
process. But the cognitive and affective states that are necessary for
concentrated reading are ones that we find hard to communicate. As a
result, the child may sit down to begin a lesson, but then daydream,
fidget, take toys from his desk, or otherwise express his activity without
doing the assignment. This type of behavior is characteristic of many
learning disabled children and can be extremely frustrating for their
teachers and parents.

Teaching the child to relax enough to be able to concentrate on learning can be facilitated with the use of biofeedback. We must recognize, however, that this is only one of the skills needed in working with a child who has a hard time learning and must be used with other learning techniques as well.

Nine-year-old Benjamin was a third grader with a diagnosed learning disability. He had been receiving remedial tutoring and attending a resource classroom as part of his schooling since the first grade. While he had mastered many of the basics of reading so that he could sound out words and even spell at an average level, Benjamin had great difficulty completing assignments because of his lack of concentration. He could work adequately with an adult on a one-to-one basis, but had not yet learned to work by himself in spite of the fact that he was reasonably well motivated and cared about getting good grades.

Before I attempted biofeedback training, I asked Benjamin simply to sit in a chair and relax. He sat in a chair looking at me; however, he was far from relaxed. He crossed his legs, crossed his arms, put his head down and then up, rolled his eyes, laughed, smiled, and did a variety of other things to get my attention. Again I told him to try to relax and asked him if he knew what I meant. Smiling and giggling he put his hands in his lap but kept his feet swaying. I then showed him a small biofeedback machine and explained to him how it worked. If he placed two fingers on the palm-sized machine, the chemicals that came from the sweat on his fingers would make the machine buzz. The more he was excited, the more the chemicals would be excited and the louder the machine would buzz. The more relaxed he was, the more relaxed the chemicals would be, and the lower the buzz would be, until the noise could not be heard. When he could hardly hear the nose, he would be relaxed, and he should stay like that for a period of five minutes.

I gave him the machine and let him try it out. During this time I explained techniques to relax his body, including deep breathing and muscle relaxation. While his fingers were lightly touching the machine, I directed him to put his feet firmly on the floor with his hands resting on his lap. I told him that he should let all his muscles relax and feel very heavy. Then, beginning with his toes, he should make each small muscle relax—first in his left foot with his large toe, then his other toes, then his arch, his heel, his calf, and his thigh, all the while breathing very deeply, and listening to the buzz as it became softer and softer. After repeating this process with his left foot and leg, we proceeded to the tips of his right fingers, up through the wrist, the forearm, and the upper arm, and then proceeded to have him relax his left fingers, hand, wrist, forearm and upper arm.

By this time the biofeedback machine reflected a significant change in Benjamin's body. No longer was he fidgeting and giggling, and his eyes were partially closed. His body was almost completely relaxed.

Next I asked him to relax the large muscles in his body—the stomach, chest, shoulders, and finally the forehead, the facial muscles, and the neck, and to continue breathing deeply and feeling relaxed. I asked him to think of someplace pleasant he had been recently, either a trip, a place near his home, or a playground—and just to remain relaxed for five minutes.

When this five-minute period was up, I told him that I would like him to complete a ten-minute reading assignment for homework and that I would leave the room and return when he was done. I knew that Benjamin could work for ten minutes at a time if he were motivated to do so. I also knew that the reading material was interesting to him and was at his level. Had I asked him to concentrate for a longer time than he was able to do, or to attempt material that was over his head, this experiment in the effects of relaxation would have surely failed.

When I returned, Benjamin had completed the assignment and was drawing a picture. He seemed to still be relaxed and calm and said that he felt so good he was able to work more quickly than he usually did.

The object of this therapy was to teach Benjamin to relax enough so that he could maximize his ability to concentrate. We worked for ten sessions, using biofeedback to get him into a relaxed state and then letting him work by himself, gradually increasing periods of time until he was able to work up to half an hour. During these ten sessions I also videotaped Benjamin working and spent time after each session reviewing the videotape with him and commenting on how well he paid attention to the work and how well he was able to sit and relax, helping him observe what it was that made him distracted from his work.

As Benjamin learned to identify when he was in a distracted state, I taught him how to use the same relaxation techniques he had used with the biofeedback machine to calm himself down and continue working. When Benjamin found that his attention was wandering and that he was doodling or daydreaming, he knew that these were signs that he was distracted; he would instruct himself to sit down, to relax, to turn over a three-minute timer, to try to achieve a "state of concentration" for those three minutes, and then go back to work.

It may be useful to review the therapeutic variables that made this particular program a success. First, there are a variety of general psychological principles that formed the structure of the program:

1. Relaxation constitutes a readiness state for focused concentration.
2. Relaxation can be taught as a conditioned response to specific external cues.
3. Children who are able to sit quietly and work are regarded as better students by their teachers than those who are more active (in spite of the fact that they may have the exact same knowledge and abilities on objective tests), and get *significantly more positive attention and praise from their teachers.*

Following the logical sequence of these principles, we can see how a relatively straightforward intra-psychic intervention can promote a behavioral change that, in turn, promotes a systems change that will potentially benefit the child's overall development. This is brief therapy at its best.

This type of program can work, however, only when we take into account the needs, abilities and interests of the child, and the resources available in his/her environment. The biofeedback instrumentation was interesting to Benjamin and made him feel that he was getting special attention. His interest in science fiction, such as Star Wars, was played upon in terms of selecting this type of treatment and in teaching him to use the equipment. The teacher and parents were kept informed of Benjamin's progress—what motivated him and what distracted him. They were encouraged to expect progress at a realistic rate and were helped to support him without being demanding. Benjamin was reinforced for success within the treatment sessions, the classroom, and at home. The reinforcement was frequent and exclusively positive.

Increasing a child's attention span is a slow process. The videotape was used as feedback to help everyone concerned with the program recognize the progress being made. When the ten sessions were done, Benjamin was given a certificate of achievement, specifying all that he had learned and emphasizing that now he could study for half an hour without supervision. I later learned that he had the certificate framed and hung over his desk at home.

Another illustration of the use of biofeedback to teach relaxation was shown with Ernest, a schizophrenic fourteen-year-old who attended a private, special education school for the moderately handicapped. Ernest, who was undergoing a variety of psychiatric treatments, was having particular trouble in his classroom because he was the scapegoat for some of the older, more aggressive boys. They would tease him about his various mannerisms, whereupon he would compulsively throw something or strike out. He would then be so upset at his own aggression that he would shake and cry and be unable to work for the rest of the day.

His teacher wondered if Ernest could be desensitized to the teasing of his classmates, and he was assigned to a psychologist under my supervision.

The psychologist designed a program that would pair relaxation with increasingly potent stimuli. Ernest would first be exposed to pictures of the boys who had teased him and then he would be told to relax. Then he would be exposed to the words the boys taunted him with (spoken by the psychologist), then to audiotape recordings of the boys' voices, and finally he would be exposed to videotape recordings of them in the classroom. (Ironically, the boys who teased Ernest were interested in helping him and fully cooperated in providing the necessary material for the program.)

But we soon found out that Ernest had no concept of what it meant to be "relaxed." He sat rigid, his eyes fixed, clenching his fists until his arms and upper body started to shake. He was taught deep breathing and progressive relaxation, but he was still so out of touch with his body that he could hardly relax for even a minute. At this time we decided to try using biofeedback with Ernest. We used a similar instrument to the one used with Benjamin; this time, however, we used visual rather than audio feedback since the buzz seemed to annoy Ernest. The visual feedback was simply a needle that registered higher when there was more agitation and lower when there was more relaxation. Rather than try to teach Ernest to monitor and reflect on his own behavior, as we had done with Benjamin, we followed a more classical conditioning approach whereby Ernest was hooked up to the biofeedback equipment throughout the desensitization training. When shown the stimulus (for example, a picture of the boys who had teased him), Ernest would tense up and react usually with some phrases like "I don't like them. They tease me. They're bad boys." Then he would be told to relax and watch the needle go down, at which time he would be instructed to remain in the relaxed state while watching the picture.

This conditioning went on for approximately a month with twice-a-week sessions. The teacher kept a record of the number of teasing incidents as well as the number of explosive outbursts that Ernest had. When Ernest was teased, the teacher would simply say, "You can relax now, Ernest," and would instruct him to sit down in a relaxed position and ignore the teasing. As Ernest learned to ignore the teasing, the boys predictably lost interest in this game and treated him more as an equal, enabling Ernest to have much more appropriate peer interaction.

For an example that demonstrates more sophisticated biofeedback instrumentation, we might look at the case of an eighteen-year-old girl, Janet, who was suffering from a number of problems, including not being able to get along with her parents, sporadic drug and alcohol abuse, poor school achievement, and migraine headaches. The headaches occurred two or three times a week, usually on school days. Janet was referred to a medical clinic that specialized in biofeedback and treating migraine headaches. Using a photoplethysometer to measure the pulse of the temporal artery, Janet watched a meter that showed the amount of blood volume in each pulse beat. Janet was told that without moving any muscles, she was to try and alternately constrict and dilate this artery for 10 minute periods. Constriction would be indicated by a lower pulse rate and dilation by a higher one. The program consisted of four weeks of treatment, two sessions per week, during which time Janet was taught how to practice this technique at home, using her finger to detect her temporal pulse.

Janet was also taught total body relaxation techniques on the assumption that these might help reduce the general tension that might bring on the headaches. By the end of the month the number of her headaches had been cut in half and the duration of the headaches cut by two-thirds. Over the next few months it was noted that Janet was able to do more homework and her grades began to improve. The successful treatment of this one symptom was a major factor in convincing her that she could learn to cope with all her problems and she became a motivated participant in individual psychotherapy.

If biofeedback is selected as the treatment of choice for a child or adolescent, care must then be taken as to what form of biofeedback is appropriate. All four of the major biofeedback modalities—GSR, Temperature, EEG, and EMG—can be used in reducing general tension, however EMG biofeedback may be the most accurate way to reduce specific stress since it can measure the tension in individualized muscle groups which vary from patient to patient.

Temperature training may be most useful in the treatment of stress reactions where the patient is primarily manifesting visceral tension (such as certain types of cardiac arhythmia, migraines, ulcers, colitis, diarrhea, and so forth), while EMG feedback may be most useful when tension is manifested in external signs, such as bruxism (teeth grinding). Although there is more controversy in the methodological problems when using EEG biofeedback, this still may be the method of choice when addressing problems associated with mental states such as sleep disorders, study problems, and emotional problems.

Bibliography

AMERICAN PSYCHIATRIC ASSOCIATION. *Diagnostic and Statistical Manual of Mental Disorders.* Third Edition. Washington, D.C.: American Psychiatric Association, 1980.

AZRIN, NATHAN and NUNN, GREGORY. *Habit Control in a Day.* New York: Pocketbooks, 1977.

BECK, AARON, RUSH, JOHN, SHAW,BRIAN, and EMERY, GARY. *Cognitive Theory of Depression.* New York: The Guilford Press, 1979.

BENSON, HERBERT. *The Relaxation Response.* New York: Avon Publishers, 1975.

BERGER, MILTON M. *Videotape Techniques in Psychiatric Training and Treatment.* New York: Brunner/Mazel, 1978.

BERNE, ERIC. *Games People Play.* New York: Grove Press, 1964.

BONGAR, B., and TAYLOR, L.P. *Clinical Application in Biofeedback.* Los Angeles: Psychology Press, 1976.

BROWN, BARBARA. *Stress and the Art of Biofeedback.* New York: Bantam Books, 1977.

BRY, ADELAIDE. *The T. A. Primer.* New York: Harper and Row, 1973.

BURNS, ROBERT, and KAUFMAN, S. H. *Kinetic Family Drawings.* New York: Brunner/Mazel, 1970.

CAMPBELL, JUNE H. *It's Me: Building Self-Concepts Through Art.* Boston: Teaching Resources Corp., 1977.

CIMINERO, A., CALHOUN, K., and ADAMS, H., eds. *Handbook of Behavioral Assessment.* New York: John Wiley & Sons, 1977.

EYSENCK, H. "A Mish-Mash of Theories." *International Journal of Psychiatry,* 70:140–146.

FEDER, ELAINE, and FEDER, BERNARD. *The Expressive Arts Therapies.* Englewood Cliffs, N.J.: Prentice-Hall, Inc., 1981.

FREED, ALVYN. *T.A. for Kids (and Grownups Too).* Sacramento, CA: Jalmar Press, 1971.

FREED, ALVYN. *T.A. for Teens and Other Important People.* Sacramento, CA: Jalmar Press, 1976.

FULLER, G. *Biofeedback, Methods and Procedures in Clinical Practice.* San Francisco: Biofeedback Institute, 1977.

GARDNER, GAIL. "Hypnosis with Children." *International Journal of Clinical and Experimental Hypnosis,* 22 (1974): 20–38.

GARDNER, RICHARD. *The Boys and Girls Book About Divorce.* New York: Bantam Books, 1970.

GARDNER, RICHARD. *The Parent's Book About Divorce.* New York: Bantam Books, 1977.

GARDNER, RICHARD. *Psychotherapeutic Approaches with the Resistant Child.* New York: Jason Aronson, 19975.

GILLIS, RUTH. *Children's Books for Times of Stress: An Annotated Bibliography.* Bloomington, Ill.: Indiana Univ. Press, 1978.

GLASSER, WILLIAM. *Reality Therapy.* New York: Harper & Row, 1965.

GREELIS, MICHAEL, and HAARMANN, BETSY. *The ABC's of Video Therapy.* Novato, CA: Academic Therapy Publications, 1980.

GURMAN, ALAN, ed. *Questions & Answers in the Practice of Family Therapy.* New York: Brunner/Mazel, 1981.

GURMAN, ALAN, and KNISKERN, DAVID. *The Handbook of Family Therapy.* New York: Brunner/Mazel, 1981.

HALEY, JAY. *Problem-Solving Therapy.* San Francisco: Harper Colophon Books, 1976.

HALEY, JAY. *Uncommon Therapy.* New York: W.W. Norton & Co., 1973.

HARRIS, THOMAS. *I'm OK, You're OK: A Practical Guide to Transactional Analysis.* New York: Harper and Row, 1969.

HARVEY, JOHN. "The Potential of Relaxation Training for the Mentally Retarded." *Mental Retardation* (April, 1979).

HERNK, RICHIE, ed. *The A to Z Guide To More Than 250 Different Therapies In Use Today.* New York: The New American Library, 1980.

HUME, W.I. *Biofeedback Research and Therapy: Annual Review.* Montreal: Eton Press, 1976.

LAMB, DEBORAH. "Life Dance: Patterns of Nonverbal Communication in Families." Master's thesis. Hahnemann Medical College, Philadelphia, Pa., 1900.

LANGE, ARTHUR, and JAKUBOWSKI, PATRICIA. *Responsible Assertive Behavior.* Champaign, Ill.: Research Press, 1976.

LAZARUS, ARNOLD. *Multi-Modal Therapy.* New York: Basic Books, 1980.

LEVICK, MYRA, et al. "The Creative Arts Therapies." *Handbook for Specific Learning Disabilities.* Edited by Adamson and Adamson. New York: Gardnor Press, 1979.

MARTIN, GARY. *Behavior Modification: What It Is and How To Do It.* Englewood Cliffs, N.J.: Prentice-Hall, Inc. 1978.

MAULTSBY, M.C., JR., and ELLIS, A. *A Technique for Using Rational-Emotive Imagery.* New York: Institute for Rational Living, 1975.

MINUCHIN, SALVADOR. *Families and Family Therapy.* Boston: Harvard University Press, 1974.

NICHOLSON, LUREE, and TORBET, LAURA. *How to Fight Fair With Your Kids and Win.* New York: Harcourt Brace Jovanovich, 1980.

OLNESS, KAREN, and GARDNER, GAIL. "Some Guidelines for Uses of Hypnotherapy in Pediatrics." *Pediatrics,* 62 (1978).

ORLICK, TERRY. *The Cooperative Sports and Game Book: Challenge without Competition.* New York: Pantheon Books, 1978.

RATHS, L., HARMIN, M., and SIMON, S. *Values and Teaching.* Columbus, Ohio: Charles E. Merrill, 1966.

SHAPIRO, LAWRENCE E. *Games to Grow On: Activities to Help Children Learn Self-Control.* Englewood Cliffs, N.J.: Prentice-Hall, Inc., 1981.

SMITH, SALLY. *No Easy Answers: Teaching the Learning Disabled Child at Home and School.* New York: Bantam Books, 1980.

SIMON, SYDNEY, HOWE, LELAND and KIRSCHENBAUM, HOWARD. *Values Clarification, A Handbook of Practical Strategies for Teachers and Students.* New York: Hart Publishing Co., Inc., 1972.

STRUNK, W.J., and WHITE, E.B. *The Elements of Style.* New York: Macmillan Publishing Co., Inc., 1979.

WOLPE, J. *The Practice of Behavior Therapy.* New York: Pergamon Press, 1969.

ZISFEIN, L., and ROSEN, M. "Personal Adjustment Training." *Mental Retardation,* 11 (1971): 16–20.

ZSWERLING, ISRAEL. "The Creative Arts Therapies as 'Real Therapies.' " *Hospital and Community Psychiatry,* 30 (Dec. 1979).

Index

Simon, Sydney, 48
sleep disturbances, 156
Smith, Sally, 123
social relationships/peer interaction,
    improving, 38
Stress and the Art of Feedback, 167
stubbornness, 66–68
symptom competition, 65
"symptomatic" behaviors, 6
"symptom removal," concept of, 6
symptom substitution, 64–65

T.A. for Kids, 44
T.A. for Teens, 44
T.A. for Tots, 44
T.A. Primer, 44
Techniques Form, 32–33
Thematic Apperception Test, in cognitive
    mediation, 80–81
therapist, as advocate of child, 9
therapy:
    criterion for conclusion, 34–35
    measuring progress of, 20
therapy plan, writing, 29
time-out room, use of, 71–72
toilet training, 58
transference, 6–7
transactional analysis (T.A.), 38, 42–47
    case, 44–47
    contraindication, 38
    indicators, 38

travel training, 142
treatment plan:
    goals and objectives, 26–28
    in hypnotherapy, 160

values clarification, 38, 47–49
    contraindication, 38
    definition, 48
    indicators, 38
Values Clarification in the Schools, 48
video self-modeling technique, 92–102
    contraindication, 92
    equipment, 95
    indicators, 92
    principles, 92–96
    techniques, 96–102
visual art therapy, 130

"warm fuzzies," 44
work adjustment, 58, 142, 152–154
writing as therapy, 124–126
written plan (therapeutic contract), 8

Young, 162

Zisfein, L., 98
Zsweling, Israel, 122, 123